Dying to Tell You

Channeled Messages from the Famously Dead

LISA NAJJAR

D1502559

For more information, contact:
Lisa Najjar
Lisa@dyingtotellyoubooks.com
www.Dyingtotellyoubooks.com

Published by Redwood Publishing

Paperback ISBN: 978-0-9975242-6-0
Ebook ISBN: 978-0-9975242-7-7

Library of Congress Control Number:
2016954339

Printed in the United States of America

Contents

Dedication

For my son:

As I raised you, you in turn raised my consciousness. Your loving heart, thoughtful actions and peaceful nature have been a gift to me and so many others. You are a truly wise and beautiful soul, Kyle. I love you ... to the moon and back.

For Ella:

Everything changed for the better when we met in that prayer circle all those years ago. You have been the visionary, mentor and champion for my life and for my Divine life purpose. I feel deep gratitude for your faith in me every step of the way. It is a privilege and an honor to have you, my dear friend, on this journey with me.

Acknowledgments

To God and my beloved angels, thank you for keeping the Light on.

Many thanks to my channeled guests for choosing me as a messenger. I feel honored.

Thank you to my long-time cherished friend and spiritual life coach, Debbie Zembal. We truly are soul sisters.

To Bob White, singer/songwriter and special friend, heartfelt thanks for allowing me to include one of your beautiful songs in my book. Mother Mary, Elvis and I agree with you – there IS only love.

To Emily Chase Smith, thank you for joining forces with me and propelling this project forward. It was "meant to be".

Thank you, Avery Auer, for your wonderful editing. You taught this proofreader a thing or two.

To David Gee, thank you for this unique cover design and great interior. You're amazing.

A huge thank you to my devoted husband, Robb. If not for you, this book would still be on my laptop! You gave me wonderful ideas, loving support, much needed structure and discipline, a kick-ass title, and plenty of hugs along the way. I couldn't have done this without you! You are my magic and my wish. You are my love.

Introduction

As Told to Emily Chase Smith, Esq.

I used to be a court reporter. Now I am reporting for a higher court—not the Supreme Court, but the Celestial Court. This is a book of channelings, messages from celebrities you know (and some you don't) from the other side, from beyond death. They came to me unsolicited, uninvited, or to use Spirit's word "unbidden," with messages of what they learned during their time on Earth, what they know now, and what they want to convey to us. Being a reporter for the Celestial Court was not a role I sought or even desired. I have always been a cheerleader, the wind beneath other people's wings—and have been happy in that role. This new role made me nervous, very nervous. Over the course of several months, I spoke to spirits and faithfully recorded their messages. And then I put them away . . . for a year.

But the spirits would not let me rest. They had a message, a message for those of us still here on Earth and they had entrusted me with that message. And so I had to move from being a mere reporter to being an ambassador. I had to step out from behind my comfortable private life with my loving husband and wonderful grown son, and into something scary. Scary, because it may not be well received and may cause people to point and laugh, scary, but the alternative is unthinkable. These messages of hope and words of wisdom from those who have been here and shared our common experience cannot stay locked inside my laptop. They must be shared, shared with those to whom they will provide help, support, encouragement, and love. And if some fingers are pointed, so be it.

Why Celebrities?

Because this project came to me unbidden, I wondered, as you may have, *why celebrities?* We know that here on Earth, once someone steps into a celebrity role, chosen or not, he or she is known to all, and thus loses his or her privacy. What I have discovered through this process is that celebrities had taken on this role *before* they came into this life. They'd had an agreement in the celestial realm to have their lives made known, and that agreement continues on the other side. They are still living in that "fishbowl" and are once again exposing their private journey to the world.

But that exposure is not only for our benefit. These celebrity spirits, whom I call "guests," have an opportunity to come back and give hopeful, helpful messages to the world, messages that bring forth a level of truth that resonates with people's hearts and souls. As you will see in this book, when some guests passed over, they were ready to be done being in the public eye, but yet they remain, invited by Spirit to use their celebrity status to share important things with the world.

Their status gives credence to their messages. That is why they were chosen and that is why we listen.

While reading, you will find different gems along the path. Not all guests or their message will resonate with you. Imagine yourself at a flower stand surrounded by one hundred different varieties of beautiful, fragrant flowers. Pick the ones you are drawn to, the ones you find particularly stunning, or ones that hold a special memory.

The channelings came to me in the same fashion and order as I have given them to you. Some people I knew of and loved. One I even shared a delightful evening with. Others, I had never heard of. Some of their messages resonated deeply and others are just beginning to become incorporated into my journey. This is a collaborative effort between me, you, and the celebrity spirits. As in all things, take what you need, and leave the rest behind.

My Experience with the Spirit World

My first experience with mediumship, although I wouldn't have known what to call it, came when I lived with a girlfriend's family at around age seventeen. The family had suffered a terrible tragedy: two of their three daughters died within two years of each other. In their home I had many experiences with the deceased girls. I would often hear them around the house and they seemed to enjoy playing little tricks on me like moving my things or hiding them. During Christmastime, laughter coming from the living room would wake me from a sound sleep, and, peeking out into the living room, I would see the ornaments on the Christmas tree moving and hear the giggling of young girls. I always spoke to them as if they were right in front of me and I think that pleased them.

In my late thirties, I saw my first medium and she came to me with a message from the other side. The message was that I could do this work also if I learned to quiet my mind to hear them. She suggested that I practice meditation. As I meditated, I began to feel a connection with the Spirit World that grew stronger each day. I took a class to learn more and found I was able to communicate with those in spirit quite easily, but I was uncertain as to whether this was the work I wanted to do in the world. While I had always prayed to be in service to humanity by helping to raise consciousness on the planet, I didn't know if this particular path was the way. To ensure that those in spirit wouldn't continue to visit me on a regular basis, I made an agreement with them. I wouldn't practice mediumship professionally, for the time being, but if a friend needed to connect with a deceased loved one, I would help.

And so it went. Quite often when I was out for a meal with a friend, I would feel the energy of someone around me. When I felt this, I knew that the visitor was a loved one coming to give a message to my companion. I would happily channel the message, feeling honored to be a bridge between Heaven and Earth.

On one occasion, I was sitting with a friend in a restaurant, and she began talking about a recent news story of an elderly couple that had gone missing while on vacation. The couple was from my friend's small town. I confessed that because I never read the paper or watched the news, I was unfamiliar with the case. As we spoke, I began to feel the presence of someone in spirit and I knew immediately that it was the missing woman. She followed me home that evening.

She stayed with me for two weeks, trying to get my attention, playing with my hair, poking me, and sitting on my bed. I heard her audibly say, "You have to find my daughter" over and over again. I told her I wanted to help, but I didn't know anything about her or her daughter. I was wondering, *How can I possibly call up a complete stranger and tell her that her missing mother is contacting me?* I began to wonder if perhaps the woman was unable to cross over into the Light. I asked if I could help her do that. She emphatically answered, "You have to find my daughter!"

I wanted to help this woman, but I didn't know how to go about doing so. More importantly, I was afraid. I stalled to gather courage. This desperate mother wouldn't leave me alone until I did as she asked. One night, I could take it no longer. I promised that the next day, I would find her daughter. That night, she asked me to get a pen and paper and I channeled a simple and sincere poem from her to her daughter and printed it on a sheet of pretty paper.

True to my word, the next day, I began my search. Fear gripped me. What if her daughter didn't believe in this type of thing? What if my message added more grief and pain to this woman that I was sure was already suffering deeply? Because it was a high-profile missing-persons case, it wasn't hard to learn the daughter's name. A friend who was familiar with the story told me she knew someone who worked with the daughter. Eventually I got her number and made the call. It was the hardest phone call I have ever made.

I said, "Hello, my name is Lisa, and I am not sure how to tell you this. Your mother has been with me for two weeks and says she won't leave until I find her daughter. I am not sure if you believe in this kind of thing, and I am not sure if you are her only daughter, but I had to contact you."

She immediately told me that she did believe in this kind of contact and wanted to know what her mother had to say. Over the phone, I began to channel a message from her mother. When I was finished, she asked if she could come over to see me.

When she arrived, I handed her the poem. She started crying and told me a story. Not long before her parents went off on their fateful holiday, she and her mother had had a conversation. She had said to her mother, "If you go before me, I want you to write me something from Heaven; that way, I will know it is you and that you are all right." She told me that she had worked with a number of psychics and mediums in an effort to locate her parents, but no one had written anything. She truly believed it was her mother reaching out to her. This experience was the first major turning point in my awareness of how meaningful this gift of mediumship could be.

After dozens of readings later for friends, I was asked by my friend Tom to communicate with his recently deceased father. Up until this point, Tom had been very skeptical about whether anyone could truly connect with those on the other side but he deeply missed his father and thought, *Why not give it a try?* As a result of the precise, poignant, and accurate message I gave him, he went from a skeptic to a believer.

Both of these experiences finally gave me confidence in my connection with the Spirit World and its ability to comfort and heal. I began to embrace and enjoy the wonderful gift that I had been given and started working as a professional medium, feeling blessed by the work that I was doing.

One of my most profound spiritual experiences was a meeting I had with Jesus. He began by showing me a movie of all types of people committing all manner of sins. There were killers, rapists, adulterers, and thieves.

In each case he asked me, "What do you see here?"

I replied, "They are perfect and beautiful." Despite their actions, while with Jesus, I saw only their true essence—their perfect and beautiful essence.

Jesus then said, "You must tell people what I have shown you here." He directed me to share this message with the world. I wondered, *What am I supposed to do next? Share this with whom? And how?* I didn't know.

My interactions with Spirit always astonished me, but none was more surprising than a visit from Walt Disney. Through a friend, Walt came to me and sang, "When You Wish upon a Star." The message was to never give up on my dream. He was referring to a spiritual television show that I was pitching at the time. He told me that if I kept on wishing and believing, it would happen, and that he would help me.

This Book

A couple of years later, Walt Disney came back. This time, he told me he had a project for me, one that would help me, as well as him. He explained that the project would help him say what he needed to say and help me to finally start down my true spiritual path. He was aware of my heart's desire to be in service to humanity and to elevate consciousness on Earth, and he was sure this project would do so. He shared that it would be a book of channeled messages from famous people. He gave me the names of some of the people I would channel, the title of the book, and showed me the book cover. I thought it was a fantastic idea, but I wasn't yet ready.

Over two years later, on Easter weekend of 2015, I was prompted, yet again, by several spirits to finally take on this project for them. This time I felt ready—and even excited! One of the first things I did was share this news with Ella, my dear friend and one of the most spiritual people I know. No sooner had I shared it with her than she fell into a deep trance and began to channel a message from Spirit for me. I watched her the entire time and saw Lincoln standing beside her. It was amazing to me! The message to me from Spirit, in part, was:

Remember the word *unbidden*. It is the most significant word for you to remember.

The telephone has been ringing, but you have not been picking it up. Pick it up! And listen!

You will be saying again and again, "Not in my wildest dreams did I ever think this would be happening. Not in my wildest dreams!"

Everything that has happened, has happened for a reason. Bringing in Tom's father, your critic and biggest skeptic, was very important; it showed you how healing this work is.

Keep all of the doubt clouds off to the side, just push them off to the side when you feel them; spirits can't get through those. They need a clear channel.

Spirit is orchestrating this whole project and lining up the people. You don't have to control it.

Evidential mediumship is important. Don't censor what you get because what you think is insignificant may not be.

If you brought this information from the pulpit or even a TV show, in a very public way, people would listen, but it would not get inside them. When they can see, read, or hear it privately, it speaks to them. It goes to their hearts.

How They Came

Although I was plagued with doubts throughout the project, and still am, I am glad this message was given to me. It has taught me, blessed me, and grown me in ways I hadn't thought possible. After receiving some messages, I felt compelled to find out more about the person with whom I'd spoken. I've included some of what I discovered in the endnotes.

Nothing was as expected while working on this project. I had no say in who came or the topic of discussion. Spirit told me they would choose the subjects and this was hard for a control freak like me. I expected sensational messages, like illegitimate babies, secret marriages, and the like, or maybe messages clearing up a mystery or two. When lovely spiritual messages came through from the celebrities, I was confused. I resonated with all of the messages and thought they were beautiful and profound, but I worried that people would expect something much more revelatory and exciting. I know that simple can be profound and that these simple truths on how to live life well were exactly what was needed in the world, but would others agree?

I reasoned that the more gossipy entertainment messages would have embarrassed and upset me to put out into the world. In contrast, the simple yet significant messages I did receive were the only type of messaging I could support. No wonder this is what the Spirit World gave to me. They knew I would align with the words being shared. These *ordinary* words were, in fact, *extraordinary*, and those with ears to hear would appreciate them.

When you look in the mirror, what you see on this day is different from what you might see tomorrow or the next day, because we see only reflections of our current thoughts and beliefs. When we move completely through the looking glass, through the mirror, we see nothing but the truth: that we are pure positive energy, free from illusions, ego, and labels. From that place of pure positive energy, we KNOW, we simply KNOW. We move from beliefs to KNOWINGS—knowings that come from the very core of our being: God, the Creator, who is Light and Love.

The messages of these guests come from that higher place, each sharing from their current level and place of awareness, more clearly than when they were attached to a body, mind, ego, and thoughts here on Earth. They have been *Dying to Tell You*. Now, let them say their peace . . .

Marilyn Monroe

April 5, 2015 — *Meadows of Relief*

I'm here picking daisies. Ah . . . I can finally return to my innocent side, my softer side.

I'm here—back home, I'd call it. There are bluebells around me.

I'm free, Lisa. Ah, I love my life here! Fields and fields of bluebells, as you call them, surround me. Sometimes I feel like I am one of these brilliant, glorious flowers, just swaying in the wind—a light, gentle breeze. That's how it feels over here. It's so gentle and warm. There's no discord, no animosity, no stress or tension.

On Earth, you go to a spa for a treatment and you get pampered, lying in a lovely room in a tranquil setting, or perhaps you are on a vacation in a beautiful place and you just have that feeling of "all is right with the world"—complete surrender and relaxation; that is how it is here, every moment of every day. Not that there are days, it's just one continuous glorious moment.

Everything is so still, so perfect, so restful.

When I was a child I always thought how wonderful it would be to live on a farm with meadows, animals, just being in nature, peaceful. I would daydream about that. But it was not to be. I guess I had other things planned for myself. But sometimes I would think about how peaceful the life of an animal was, and wish I could be that. No worries. Just being. Not doing, just being. Like the flowers, they just "are."

It exhausts me, just looking back over my lifetime, replaying the days there. I feel utterly exhausted going over it. I'm not sure how I even survived.

I'm showing myself to you as I was when I was famous, but that was just a mask I wore. Ah . . . to be free of that!

I wasn't ready for all of that. It really took it out of me!

They shouldn't let kids act like grown-ups. They should be protected. Kept safe. There was no one keeping me safe. I was like a child thrown into the role of head of the family. When all I knew was . . .

[She showed me the flowers around her.]

I went a little off course, I would say. I wanted out much sooner than I got out. Ha! It was all too much.

It's a hard life down there. Here, we can wear white and stay in the meadow all day long if we want to. No one calls us. There is certainly no time, no watches, and no schedule. It's very peaceful and relaxing.

I took a big, long break when I first arrived here. Not everyone does, but I needed to. I was exhausted. So tired. It's just not how people would think it is. It's not a walk in the park; believe me. I longed for simpler times, for simpler days, for simpler moments, and here I have them. So you can imagine that I'm not in any rush to get back there now. I am content to lie in the flower fields and just let myself be.

My young body was all worn out. Such a pity. That should not have been. Ha! You like to say, "There are no *shoulds*," so I will refrain from using that phrase. There really aren't any shoulds here, though, just wants.

I suspect, when I do decide to come back, I will choose a very different life. I will have children. I missed that opportunity this time around and it caused a sadness for me. In my next life, I will have lots of friends and deep connections with many people. I will have simple experiences and relationships based on deep connection and love. Two ends of the spectrum, two lives.

[*Marilyn took a deep breath.*]

So relaxed. It's just so peaceful here, truly. I can walk in my bare feet and no one looks at me funny. I can just be myself.

I'm showing myself to you as I was in the white dress, but I am just a little girl now. We can be any age we want to here.

It's so beautiful. I love walking among the flowers. They tickle my legs. No more work, no more anything, just the most indescribable freedom! Wow! If you only knew—but I suspect you do—how exquisite everything is here! How full of joy it is. There is a vibration here that is not found on Earth. It might burn you up if it was there. Cool water, peace, gentle breezes, joy, freedom, and deep, deep love are mine here.

I can see that you, Lisa, are really feeling me, and that is good. Can you feel your body completely relax as you step into mine? Of course, I'm smiling because I don't have a body anymore, so I really ought to say, "Step into my Light." Can you feel how every part of you relaxes when you enter the vibration that I am in now?

Being on Earth is so fantastic, so extraordinary, such a one-of-a-kind experience that nothing really compares to it. And because of this, one must enjoy all that the Earth has to offer, and there are plenty of things the Earth has to offer! It's the place where we get to taste and smell and laugh and cry, to remember and to forget, to sing, to dance, to play. There are so many joys there—oh, so many joys to be had on Earth. But for as many beautiful high and joyful experiences, there are equally deep and dark canyons. That's the fun of it! It really is! Well, I see that now.

When I was there, I was ill-equipped to handle what life threw at me and all I wanted was out. I needed to get out! It was ripping me apart: the people, the pressure, never being seen, not really.

I'm not sure what I was even supposed to learn there. I haven't been shown, not yet. I haven't learned that yet here. I don't know why that all happened. I just know that I bit off more than I could chew, as the saying goes.

That isn't to say, though, that my choice was correct: drowning myself in escapism and drugs. It was not the way.

What little time I have had on Earth was blocked. I had so few years without my "mask" on. Oh, *do* we wear them—on Earth, that is—but here, no need. Everybody here is his or her own truth.

If I had known then what I know now, I would've taken some of this truth there and used my celebrity status to help people, to bring joy, to bring light, to bring truth. But I didn't know, and that's OK. Look at me now; it's never too late, is it?

I don't want to stay long because I have some living to do! But I do think it is very important to share what little more I do know now.

Feel with your whole heart. Play with reckless abandon. Lie in the meadow. Don't miss an opportunity to tell someone he or she means the world to you.

Babies are precious and they get a lot of attention. Everybody loves a baby. But did you know that teenagers are babies too, and moms are babies too, and grandmas are babies too? Underneath the appearance, there is a spirit—a lovely, sparkling, full-of-joy Light that is trying to get out. It wants to come out. It needs to come out. So let the Light come out! Let the child play at any age, at every age.

Appreciate where you are because you are not long for that place. It all happens so fast. It's as if one minute, you're there and the next, you're here. Even if you live a long, long life, it's still hardly anything, so never try to rush any process. That saying, "Stop and smell the roses," well, that is really true. I lie in meadows filled with flowers all day long now. I never want to get up. I do get up, but seldom. I just want to lie and lie and lie in the fields—the flower fields. There is nothing more.

[*As she said, "There is nothing more . . ." I thought she was going to say, "Nothing more important than . . ." or "There is nothing more something than . . ." but I waited and waited and then felt her retreat.*]

ENDNOTES:

After buying her first home in 1962, Marilyn became an avid and enthusiastic gardener—happily buying plants, shrubs, and trees for her yard—and spent a lot of time gardening.

In an interview she gave in the weeks before her death, she suggested to *Life* magazine that she was tired of fame. Of her notoriety, she said, "It might be kind of a relief to be finished."

At their 1954 wedding (according to biographer Donald Spoto), Monroe asked DiMaggio whether, should she die first, he would decorate her grave with fresh flowers every week, as William Powell had done for proto–platinum-blonde bombshell Jean Harlow after her tragically early demise. DiMaggio said he would, and even though he had been long divorced from Monroe when she died in 1962, he made good on the promise for the next twenty years.

Abraham Lincoln

April 8, 2015 — *Live and Let Live*

When one comes in to abolish slavery, one has a very important job. I did not act on my own, however; the company of Heaven acted with me. It was a great collaboration. Tell those on the Earth plane; have them know that they are guided in every step that they take. Their guardian angels, angels, teachers, they all work with them.

I knew from the time I was a young boy that I was here for a very important purpose. I saw the slaves and I knew even then that they were my brothers and sisters. I had a burning desire—*a burning desire*—to right this wrong and to bring people together as one.

People look at me and remember me as someone very special. I can assure you, I am not special. The fire that burned inside of me also burns inside of you. You're all light of the eternal flame and there is no action that is insignificant or unworthy or pointless. There is no word that is small. Every single thing that we think about, act on, and speak about reverberates for all of time and space.

I was chosen as one messenger but understand this: You are all messengers. You all have a job to do. You all have light to share. You all have love to give.

Lighten the burden of your fellow man. Relieve the sorrow of your brother. Give all that you have.

I will oversee this project. It holds great fascination for me. When I was on Earth, I consulted with mediums, as did my wife. Many did not understand this, but I knew, even as a child, that there are more things unseen than seen. I was very connected to the heavenly realms. This formed part of the deep bond my wife and I shared.

The message that I have to impart to you is that you are all special. Not one among you is less special. If only you could understand that.

Stand in the power that you are. Stand for peace, for unity, and for love.

I may have drafted a famous document, but you are living it. It takes more courage to live it every day. It takes much more courage.

You cannot see the soul of another. The other can appear as an enemy and yet you must treat him as if he were yourself. Only in so doing will your soul light up from the inside. It was a difficult time when I lived. There was so much fear and hatred and darkness. The world was not looking for the light. It was steeped in covers of darkness. It was a dark and dismal time, but one ripe with opportunity.

Oh, how wonderful is your light, pouring into the darkness! The richness of your souls is beyond comprehension. Every soul is like a brilliant diamond. It is treasure so rare that it should be guarded around the clock.

If you could see each other with the eyes of your heart, what a wondrous world would you live in.

Take up your cause today! You are here but for a short time, so make the most of it! Leave a legacy of love. Shine light on everyone around you. Revel in laughter and in all things. Be true to yourself.

When you come onto this side of the veil, it is only your light that distinguishes you from another. Make that light as dazzling as you can!

Kindness matters. Forgiveness matters. Truth matters.

I have said enough now. I will return because I am overseeing this project.

What I have said here today is of utmost importance.

Live and let live.

ENDNOTES:

I thought "Live and let live" was a modern saying. In my research, I discovered that Catharine Sedgwick (1789–1867) wrote the book *Live and Let Live* in 1837. Lincoln was twenty-seven years old when the book was published. Her books were in high demand from the 1820s to 1850s.

Waylon Jennings

April 14, 2015— *It's About Time*

You're smiling because my line is in one of your favorite movies, isn't it? That's right; yes, I am dead! I have to say this because you don't know whether I am or not. You are actually asking that question right now in your head: *Is he dead?* Yes, ma'am, I am dead. As dead as they come . . . as dead as it gets, ha-ha-ha-ha!

This is fascinating, what you are up to. I am honored to be part of it.

They came and got me one morning, although there aren't any mornings where I am. It's just one continuous Light, as radiant as your most brilliant sunshiny day. It's always this way, unless, of course, you want to see the darkness. Then you will.

So they came to get me one day, ha-ha-ha—as if there are days! See, where I am there's no time. Nope, none at all. It's a lot like Earth and it's nothing at all like Earth. Whatever it is that a person wants to see, he can see. It's like having a blank canvas and you can draw whatever you want on it and you can paint whatever you want on it. It's quite wonderful! So how do you want to see the afterworld? If you dream it, you can see it and you can experience it. It's all in the mind.

They came to get me and they asked me if I wanted to be part of "Project Earth." I laughed. "Quite a bit, actually!" I said. "Sure, why not?" I headed down—yes, down—to a place almost like a recording studio . . . interesting. Maybe they thought that it would be something special for me, being from the music industry, of course. And it is! This is really fantastic! So I'm in this sort of sound studio like I'm about to cut a record, and a few of the glowing white beings came to explain that I was to have a conversation with you for a book.

Well, what would you like to know, ma'am?

Lisa: What is the most important thing you learned when you went to the other side?

The thing that I learned very quickly when I came here was that there's no need to hurry! While I was on Earth, it was always hurry, hurry, rush here, rush there, get things done, don't waste time, be on time. Time! Time! Time! Such emphasis on *time!* Annoying, almost.

Well, I can tell you all now that it's a big farce, the "time" thing! Ha-ha! Not only does it not exist, but also, the preoccupation with it robs time from the things that are truly important. It takes you from the sole reason you are in a body in the first place!

You are not on Earth to run from this activity to the next, to the next, to the next. You just run right into the grave that way, running willy-nilly everywhere and nowhere at the same time. You run yourself into an early grave!

What I would suggest is to find the things that are very, very important to you—maybe your home, your friend, your child, dancing, whatever it is that lights up your spirit, the thing that brings so much joy into your life—and just be with that, really be with that.

Don't think about time when you're doing those things—loving that child, singing that song, lying in that grass. Just know in those moments that thing is the reason for your very creation! It is the most important thing you will ever do! Lie in that grass. Talk to that child. Throw your head back and twirl around that dance floor. It is in living those moments that you truly live! There's nothing really more important.

I did not know this, like many of you. And so while I was a "gifted artist," I never enjoyed the song. I never enjoyed the song, Lisa.

There is no such thing as regret over here, but if there were, I'd have it for that reason: for missing the song. Everyone enjoyed my songs except for me. It seems as if I lived my life for the rest of the world to enjoy, not for me. I had no time to feel the music, to sing the song.

So whatever it is you're doing that brings a smile to your face, a twinkle to your eye, a warm feeling to your heart, a tap to your toe, be in it! Enjoy the wonder of being human!

So, you see, when I tell you from this perspective that sitting and talking with the child, lying in the grass, dancing your dance is so important to be present with, you can see it's the simplest things that you will miss the most when you get over here, where I currently reside.

I am not sure if I will be allowed to come back and talk anymore with you. So I will say my farewell. I can see they are calling me back through the curtain and it will close on me. Thank you for thinking me so important that you would include me in this dialogue. I feel honored.

Walt Disney

April 18, 2015 — *Life Through a Child's Eyes*

Come take a ride with me, Lisa, on this beautiful star-filled blanket of Light. What a magical time I am having here! It's truly spectacular! If you think Disneyland is amazing, just wait till you get here!

The problem with most people is that they give up. They give up before they even begin. Their minds are wide open when they're children and teenagers and even young adults, then something happens and they shut down.

Oh, to keep the wonder of a child! That's what I was able to do. That was the only difference between me and some other folks. I could see things through the eyes of my child. It's not impossible; everyone can do this. If they could push the worry clouds off to the side just for a little while, they could see this magic star-filled carpet we are on right now.

Your life there is not supposed to be like that. It's not supposed to be drudgery and hardship and stress. I do not believe that was ever the plan.

It's not easy to walk around looking through the eyes of your child (and by that, I mean your *inner* child). I understand how difficult it really is in your third dimension. The whole world is out to keep you down, to keep you struggling and blocked. Yes, to keep you limited. There is a way out, right in front of you. Open your eyes and look. The trap is only in your mind.

When you look with the eyes of a child, you are able to fly to magical places. Oh, the things that you can create from that place! Your imagination will soar and you will be filled with the belief that you can do it! In fact, there would be no opposing beliefs within you. How do you think I wrote what I wrote, designed what I designed, created what I created?

I know many of you reading this will ask yourselves, *but how? How can I see the world through my child's eyes?* You are asking, *How is it possible to do this when I have so much responsibility and weight on my shoulders?* I am here to tell you that in the very moment that you cross over into this dimension, you will be freed. You will wonder what took you so long to shrug it off.

What I am saying is that you can decide to shrug it off now! You can enjoy that state of being while you are still in the earthly body. You can enjoy it, play with it, create from it. Is there a dream that you have? Are there any wishes that are unfulfilled in your life? It is time to follow the dream. Make the wish and watch it come true.

Believe in yourself. Believe in the goodness of the universe. Believe that you have support from the heavens. With your will and your dream, all is possible!

Now, a little about this place. It is just magical—a 24/7 amusement park! You see, it's whatever you wish. Anything your mind decides it wants, it can have. And for me, I wanted amusement parks, rides, cotton candy, play, laughter, song. And I know that when I finish here, when I've had enough, I will move on.

I have been riding these rides since I arrived here and it's been a thrill. I ride with the young children that cross over. They spend a long time in this beautiful, thrilling, joyous Candyland.

The children adapt very quickly, much more so than the adults and the elderly. They really know where they're going. They are not afraid.

So I continue making children smile, even here, with my Candyland.

When children come over here they are perfectly fine. But because their parents do not think they are fine and grieve them so, the children stay connected to Earth. They wait and watch until their parents are able to let them go. They wait for as long as they need to. As they wait they have fun, though. They can keep an eye on their parents and siblings while they play and enjoy the amusement park I have created.

So, parents, just know that your children are in Divine hands. They laugh and they play and they are fully alive in this place. Their only sadness is watching you suffer. They will not leave you alone.

Your children fly free here in the same way that they did before they were born to you. This is their true home, as it is yours.

If you could allow them to fly in this way, it would truly set them free. This is not to say, dear parents, that you cannot miss them or wish them back with you. Yes, love them and miss them, while you set them free. This is the greatest gift that you can give them. Allow them to play. Allow them to soar. Allow them to giggle and laugh and be more alive than they ever were on Earth. If you could see them here, how happy they are, you would most certainly do this. It is a very difficult thing that I am asking you to do, but a most important thing.

Now I wish to speak about passion. For all of you still in the third dimension, live your life with passion! Do everything with passion! Swim in it. Play in it. Wrap yourself up in it. Roll around in it. It just makes life so much better!

You all had it at one time. Do you remember? Do you remember having passion in all that you did? Wasn't life just that much more fun? Well, it can be again! Go through life with zest and joy and passion! We are on Earth for such a short time. Why waste even a moment of it in apathy, in ordinariness?

Keep your mind on the things that bring you the most joy. Do this, and I can guarantee your life will improve tenfold.

This is one of the hardest things for me to see when I peek through the curtain. I sometimes wish that I could shout down from the heavens, "Lighten up! Smile! Do the things that bring you the most joy! Surround yourself with people who bring you joy! Watch programs that bring you joy. Read books that bring you joy. Then you will have a joy-filled life!"

It is time for me to go now. I hope that some of the things that I have talked about here today will stay with you. I urge you to dream, and risk, and seek joy in all that you do. For then, it will be Heaven on Earth for you.

Elvis Presley

April 21, 2015 — *There Is Only Love*

Howdy! This is wonderful! Thank you!

It's so good to have a connection to that place. I miss it!

I've been asleep for a very long time. With all the substance filling up my system, I needed time to rest and restore myself, to clear out the garbage—not only the physical garbage, but the mental garbage as well. I died with a head full of confusion and doubt and sadness and remorse and pain. That takes time over here to clear. It's like waking up from a long, long sleep when you finally do. Don't worry; you won't have to go through what I did. Your body isn't full of poison.

I guess I needed to rest. My life was not easy or ordinary. I asked for that life, thought it would be idyllic—far from it!

I went off course in so many ways. My relationship with everyone and to everything was damaged by the time I departed. I loathed myself at the end. I couldn't stay in and I couldn't get out. What a place to be, "eh"? That's a little Canadian for you, Lisa! So I checked out. It was the only way I could cope. In fact, I checked out long before I officially did. I just wasn't present anymore and certainly not enjoying my "idyllic" life.

I could have done SO much with my position in that lifetime. So much! If I had known what I know now, I'd have made my time there count. Oh, the money and the name—how they could have helped others!

I'm in a space here where I'm more aware of what is happening. I'm able to see my lifetime frame by frame. While I see that I brought much happiness to the world through my music, I feel some sadness and regret.

Those on this side, at least where I am, just love me. Thoroughly. There is only love surrounding me here. It's only me that judges me. I know that when I finish with this little "pity party" of mine, I will go with the pure heavenly beings that surround me to a place beyond sorrow. For now, though, I am here.

My heart weeps a little for actions undone, and actions done. To have destroyed myself when I had so much to offer the world just feels very, very heavy. For how long I will stay this way, I don't know. Until I'm done, I suppose, and ready to see with a clearer perspective.

[*I started feeling so sad and heavy. I could see his head down and his shoulders slumped. I started to cry, feeling him.*]

Cherish life: that is my message.

Cherish your body; it is a gift.

Lisa, I see you are sad because you, yourself, struggle so much with this. I implore you, everyone, to look at your body and your life as a treasure—a treasure chest of jewels. So precious. So magnificent. So extraordinary. So special.

Do all that you can with your body—and your life.

Make a difference in the world. It doesn't have to be the whole world; it can be one person. Because that person IS the world. That person is YOU.

Be kind.
Offer a hand.
Accept the limitations of others and love them anyway.
Be patient.
Be a friend.
Change the world, one person at a time.

Because from what I can see here . . . ahhh, what you do for one resonates throughout all of eternity—*all of eternity!* It is magnificent! If you could see from down there, what I can see from up here, you would "do kindness" all day long. You would help someone up, offer him a hand, and put his needs first.

This "kind-doing" has a vibration that circles the world—the entire world! It then radiates off the planet, into space, reaching all worlds, all galaxies, all solar systems, all dimensions of time and space. Oh, it makes me cry to think about it.

Just one "love offering" to another is the stuff that worlds are created from—heavenly, high-minded worlds.

[Even though I was on an airplane, I was overwhelmed by his sadness and couldn't stop my tears from falling.]

Can you understand what I am saying? I am saying that every movement of your hand sets off an energetic chain of events that ripple out into eternity!

Can you imagine what the world would be like if each of you "did kindness?"

[I felt true peace wash over me—peace and satisfaction. I was feeling him.]

That is the most important message I can leave you with. It's not newsworthy to some, but absolutely the key to life lived well. When I speak of life, I am referring to ALL life—eternal life. Make no mistake about it, you will take yourself and all that you are, all that you've done, all that you've said and thought, with you.

It is a loving place that I am at. There's no judgment whatsoever, except my own of myself. They are helping me leave that behind so that I can advance in Light levels.

I don't feel that I will stay here long, just long enough to really feel my emotions. For so much of my life, I didn't feel my emotions. This is as good a time as any to finally do this. So don't worry about me. I am clearheaded and prepared to complete this part of my journey. I am loved beyond words here in this place, not because I'm famous or wealthy or talented. No, I am loved here because I AM. I now, finally, feel blessed.

Good-bye, Lisa. It was such a pleasure and a gift to speak through you today. You felt me. Blessings to you and yours.

[A song, "Psalm to Mary" played over and over inside my head during the entire visit with Elvis.]

I like the song. I want it included here.

Lisa: If you want it in, Elvis, then it's in.

Yes, I want it in.

[I thought we were through and I was putting my notebook away, when I felt a presence. I thought perhaps he had come back to add something more, but I soon realized it was Mother Mary. She was there, caressing my face with so much love. She filled my heart with love. I could barely keep the tears from streaming down my face. Because I was on the plane, I wanted to resist her so as not to embarrass myself, but she continued on, filling my heart with love, breaking it open. And she said to me in the most beautiful voice I'd ever heard, "There IS only love." As she left me, I heard Elvis say, "It's my sentiment exactly!"]

ENDNOTES:

"Psalm to Mary"

I've read the Bhagavad Gita
Proverbs and Psalms
The Gospel of Thomas
And Kahlil Gibran
You think I'd know by now
But I forget somehow

I've turned the tarot
I've rolled the I Ching

Played with numbers and planets
Crystals and beads
You think I'd know by now
But I forget somehow

I seen the mighty Pacific
And the other side too
I perched with a raven
In Malibu
You think I'd know by now
But I forget somehow

I been to Taos and Sedona
Walked the white Gulf sands
Climbed a cold hoodoo
In the Alberta badlands
You think I'd know by now
But I forget somehow
Mary, My Mother
Mother Mary
Mary, My Mother
Mother Mary

I've watched three babies leap into the world
I've watched them wonder, suffer, and toil
You think I'd know by now
But I forget somehow

I've known the pain of too much tenderness
I've been wounded in love, buried in bliss
You think I'd know by now
But I forget somehow
Mary, My Mother

Mother Mary
Mary, My Mother
Mother Mary

I'm blessed and I'm broken
Like a shipwreck
She asks me for money
I write her a check
You think I'd know by now
But I forget somehow

There's nothing but love
You're either out or you're in
But I keep forgetting
Again and again
You think I'd know by now
But I forget somehow
Mary, My Mother
Mother Mary
Mary, My Mother
Mother Mary
Mary, My Mother
Mother Mary
Mary, My Mother
Mother Mary

Steve McQueen

April 24, 2015 — *Ride the Wave with Gusto*

I feel so timid; this is really strange. Never knew this could be done.

I hope I do this right. Is there a right way? I always strove to be right, do everything right. I guess I still do.

I miss Earth. I truly do. I know I'm supposed to be in "Heaven" and I am, and it's a fine place, just fine, but I was not ready to go yet. I long to be back.

What a ride it was for me! I had so much--so much love, so much excitement, so much of everything. Excess, you might say, and that's okay.

We are only down there for the ride. What a thrilling ride I took! I feel like I'd trade places with almost anyone down there, just for another shot at living! Well, maybe not anyone! I'd like a good life, exciting, you know.

I liked living on the edge! I liked driving fast cars and flying fast planes. I did everything to the max. All the way, baby! I really used my life to the fullest. Didn't waste a sec.

I miss my wife. I watch her, and I so much wish I could be down there with her. Being with a woman, one you truly love, is the icing on the cake of a good life! You know what I mean? It's the bomb!

And my kids. I miss each one of them. I don't take my eyes off any of them. I try to help them from here, as I am allowed, of course. There's only so much you can do from here. I can't interfere with their free will. But let them know, Lisa, that I am walking every step alongside them. You know what it is to love a child, so you will understand how difficult it is for me to be parted from them.

It's just so lonely here without them. I'm told it doesn't have to be and I'm urged to move on into happier spheres. But for now I just want to stay here, lamenting what I've left behind. I'm simply not ready to move on to anywhere else.

So I relive my days down there, feel all my experiences, play back all of my magic moments. It's MY Heaven—MINE.

To my children, I am not sad, just missing you all. I want to be at the table with you when you gather. I want to be at all your events. "I don't wanna miss a thing," as the other Steve sings [Tyler]. Pains me that I have to miss anything, but thank God I don't have to completely miss out! I can see so much from here. And hear your thoughts and prayers and hear your hearts beat. I stay so close to my loved ones, especially my son, who seems to need me most. He will know who he is. I hear your longings and feel your pain and I comfort you how I can. Can you feel me, my son?

Life has its ups and downs; that is a fact. Even the downs, though, beat not being there! It's just such a ride—such an incredible ride, Earth is!

Ride the waves and the roller coaster with gusto! Give it all you got, for heaven's sake. You'll have plenty of time to rest once you get here.

You're feeling some of those ups and downs right now, aren't you, Lisa? [*There was turbulence on the plane right then.*] And that's the stuff that life's made up of! Ride them with courage and a thrill-seeking attitude! Makes everything grand!

I'd love to be flying on that plane with you, Lisa. Love to be flying it! I loved to fly, as do you. When I would hit turbulence, I'd get excited; it meant that things were gonna get exciting. That's how I looked at all of life. When the turbulence hit, it became a really fun ride! I sure didn't like things staid and settled. No, not me.

Acting—and all of Hollywood life—was like that, thrilling and bumpy like a giant roller coaster; that's why I loved it.

And even if I hadn't "made it," I'd have loved it all the same. Because it IS the journey! It's the ride! The twists and turns and uncertainties and setbacks and challenges and successes form the whole picture, add to the whole drama of it all.

Oh God, how I miss it! Here we can experience anything we want and so I guess I can recreate a life. But I'm happier watching scenes from my past life—and my family's present one.

I feel somewhat tired now. I feel I've said enough. I'm not sure I've said anything profound here, but I shared honestly. And that's all I can do.

Enjoy those bumps, Lisa. Don't shy away from them and pray for relief. Just ride up one side of them and down the other. It'll add layers of fabric to your life's quilt.

I'm slipping back to where I'm stationed for the time being. It was so interesting, doing this. May I come again?

Lisa: Yes.

Thank you. And if you don't mind, I'll follow your ride now too, Lisa, if that's OK?

Lisa: Yes, sure, Steve. How kind. Thank you. Blessings to you.

Mother Mary

April 29, 2015 — *Drop into Your Heart*

[I felt the sweetest, gentlest energy floating around me.]

Lisa, open up your heart. Just let it open. Don't be scared. Did you see how Kendale [*a friend*] was this weekend? When he stopped distracting himself and filling himself up with activities, he felt. You saw that, I know. He softened. He was present. That is what people should remember, how sweet life can be when you live from your heart.

The activities that fill the days of most people are just that, fillers. They fill in the pain holes. There are places in everyone where pain resides. Sometimes it sits in deep dark caverns like the Grand Canyon. Other times, it's like armor all around someone. Either way, the pain sits there. It's still. No one wants to disturb it. It's like sweeping out a garage. When the broom first starts sweeping, the dust flies everywhere. It's dirty and difficult to avoid, the dust.

Pain is like that. If you begin to disturb it, to peek in at it, pull the cover off the pain, it starts to make a mess. Not many people want the mess. There seems to be no time to clean it up. So they prefer to leave it as is. But it doesn't feel good, just sitting there. It pokes at you, nudges you. It starts to irritate.

So what do you do? Y'all ignore it. Y'all drink (you liked "y'all" so much in Tennessee). Y'all shop, work, watch TV, sleep, take pills, get depressed, pray. You do everything except feel. Feeling scares so many of you.

Do you realize that it doesn't have to be the way you think it does? You do not have to go crawling around all the dark corridors of your psyche, unearthing all of your shadows and ghosts, healing and transforming. No, it is much simpler and sweeter than that. You simply have to "drop into your heart." You like that phrase, don't you, Lisa? You've been using that a lot lately.

That, though, is the only answer. If people dropped into their hearts, always, all their pain would subside; their fears, disappear; their problems, vanish. They would live in the energy of God. They would float on clouds of goodness and joy.

Try it. When you are stressed about something, in that moment, think of someone or something that causes your heart to fill with love. How do you feel now? Does anything else matter now or are you simply resting in the palm of God's hand? You are. That is where you belong.

Do this often. Again and again, you will experience this bliss place. The more you do it, the more you will want to do it. If you do it enough, it will become your "go to" place. It will be your first place. The vibration that will surround you when you are in that place will affect all those around you, your environment itself. It's like you'll be bringing a spa with you wherever you go, complete with the ambient, meditative background music.

It's a very simple exercise. Please try it. See how it changes your lives.

Feel, all of you, not pain and regret and anger, but feel love. It will bring you directly to joy and inspiration. It's like being on the top of a mountain, looking out over the most beautiful vista. Reside there, as often as you can. Y'all will be happy you did.

[*I saw three hearts; she wanted me to have them.*]

Tennessee Williams

April 29, 2015 — *The Other Side of Change*

Oh boy, what a trip this is! Ha-ha! I can't believe I'm one of the people called to this project. Oh my! What should I talk about? Seems we've covered love, and time, and being present, and passion, and regret. I'd like to talk about change.

They say that the only thing you can be certain of is change. That is really true. Just in my lifetime alone, the changes were staggering: technology, advancements, consciousness, social climate.

So many people shy away from change because they're afraid. I say, dive into it! The gems are on the other side of the change—new adventure, the unknown, the mystery. That's life! When you trust that you are residing with God and that nothing can ever go wrong, you will look forward to change. It is when we do not have faith, when we believe that we are at risk somehow of loss or of death, that we avoid, resist, and block change, but it comes anyway.

Do you know why we go to the Earth? For change. That's right. We actually go down there to experience change.

Are you surprised? There would be no point without change. Now, some like to call it "evolution," or "enlightenment," or "growth." I will stick to the word "change," because I like it. When we are in the other realms, say, where I am, there is also growth, evolution, and change, but when we are on the Earth we get to *live* the change! We get a chance to embody the change, to experience the change. It is a live, visceral, full experience!

We could've just stayed right here, resting on clouds with harps playing. It's true; we could've, after all. We have that choice. As a matter of fact, we choose everything. But here's the interesting thing: we never choose to stay here. No, we want the Earth experience. And what is the Earth experience? Change.

Life on Earth is so very rich. It's unique. It's sublime. It is rich with texture, color, and dimension.

I loved change when I lived. I looked for opportunities to change things. I got a high from it. I'm not saying that I knew something that others didn't. I'm sure there are lots of people who enjoy change, but so many don't.

I speak now to those who are afraid of change: When life throws you curveballs, know that those are your greatest opportunities to evolve. The things that you do not plan, that "get in your way"—the things that make you stumble, fall, lie down—those places in life are where the juice is! If you can reframe those events, you will then begin to make the most out of these glorious opportunities coming your way.

It was said on another day to "ride the waves." I believe Steve McQueen said that and I am repeating it. Ride the waves! Don't look back, only forward. The blessings are ahead, the learning is ahead, and the joy is ahead!

Sometimes you can't see all of this at the beginning, or even during or at the end of a specific change, but I am here to tell you that your soul sees it. It knows it, and feels it, and registers it, and records it. It is why you live.

It's been said that life is short and, oh, is that true! You've set up opportunities and challenges for yourself. They're growth opportunities. So just know that when they come, you have planned them. You have painstakingly designed those changes, every last detail of them, before you arrived on Earth. Just know that they were created especially for you—by you. They were set up in order to grow your soul.

Does that help you? Does it help, knowing that you created all of those supposed obstacles? That they serve you? Your higher self knew this, knew that it would serve you, so it was set up to do so.

My life had so many sharp edges, so many ups and downs. I sometimes felt like I lived upside down! It's funny, though; I suppose I knew deep, deep down that all of it was for my higher good and growth. And so I made the most of it. I almost looked forward to the changes, to the upsets and the setbacks, to the downfalls. I suppose I could've been called a masochist, but I just enjoyed the challenge of getting up again, not unlike a fighter in the ring. To fall and get up, to fall and get up, to fall and get up—what strength, courage, fortitude and faith we call up in ourselves when we do this. It's really something!

And I tell you this: when you cross over to this side and you sit in your recliner and watch your life review with a drink in one hand, and a remote control in the other, you will eagerly look for those places in your drama where you had the most adversity. It will be the highlight of your movie, believe it or not!

So, in closing, I would say that the next time you fall on your knees, begging to know why this bad thing has happened to you, just imagine yourself in that recliner, popcorn in hand, on the edge of your seat, just waiting to see what unfolds next in your life. Imagine yourself sitting in suspense, watching what you did next.

Make it a good one—the movie, that is! That's really what it's about. It's the only game in town! Thank you so much for allowing me to share my two cents. I hope my words help in some way.

Good day and peace to all.

ENDNOTES:

I am embarrassed to admit that I did not know who Tennessee Williams was; I was thinking of Hank Williams the country singer. In my research I discovered he was a playwright—no wonder the movie reference! I also learned that in order to stimulate his writing, he moved often to various cities including New York, New Orleans, Key West, Rome, Barcelona, and London. Williams wrote, "Only some radical change can divert the downward course of my spirit, some startling new place or people to arrest the drift, the drag."

Paul Newman

May 2, 2015— *True Love Never Dies*

I miss my wife and my children so much. There is so much love in my heart that it's hard for me to even talk to you.

I just want to take some time to let you, Lisa, feel these feelings I have for my family. Can you feel how much I love them?

Lisa: Yes, I can. [I could feel deep love in my heart. I just let him overshadow me in a way that really allowed me to tap into his feelings.]

She took my breath away from the first time I saw her. It was like springtime in the middle of winter.

You just don't know happiness until you love somebody with all of your heart. I wouldn't have traded any of my success, money, or experiences for the love that I felt for my wife. It meant so much more to me than any other thing I could have had or enjoyed on Earth. Kids today, unfortunately, have this idea that marriage is temporary. There's even a term now that's popular: "starter marriage."

I'm not here to say that everyone has to have a lifelong marriage—far from it. I can see that there are many times and instances in which it is better to move on from one spouse and, in order to have another experience in a different way with a different person, sometimes that's the best thing. Perhaps the learning is done and you need a new set of circumstances to help you grow to the next level.

But if you are lucky enough to find a mate who you love with all your heart, who you respect, who you admire, who you adore, who you enjoy, then hold on tightly; never let her go.

Keep the romance alive. Never stop telling her how much she means to you. It's essential.

There's so much temptation, so much choice in the world, so much stimulation, so much activity, so many options, that it is difficult to keep your eye on the prize and keep focused on the one you love. But truly, if you can, it is a blessing beyond words! To grow together in love is absolutely the richest experience you can have.

But, as I am sure most people have learned, it does take effort and the will to keep the fire burning brightly. It doesn't just magically happen, although I am sure there are some couples for whom that is the reality. However, in most cases, it takes time, nurturing, desire, and will to keep the bond strong.

Some relationship tips from me? I am no expert, but I have a few. Especially from up here, I can see quite clearly where I went wrong, what I could have done differently, and so I think I can share a few tips that I believe will help you.

Never go to bed angry. It's in all of your pop-psychology books, and it's true. Do whatever it takes. Sit up all night if it means getting yourselves to a point where you want to hold one another. Just knowing that you are not allowed to go to bed angry is inspiration enough to get to the heart of the matter quickly and deal with it.

Never, never, never let a disagreement carry over into the next day. Find a way to meet in the middle somewhere. Agree on how you will handle things the following day. Perhaps schedule an appointment with a marriage counselor. Have a plan when you go to sleep and then hold each other tight.

Compliment each other often. This just brings a smile to my face— to my spirit face. Tell your partner what you love about her! No one ever tires of hearing wonderful things said about oneself! That's one area in which overdoing it is a good thing!

Make your partner feel like the most important person ever, the most special person ever. She IS that special! Appreciate her. Appreciate what she brings to your life. Appreciate what she does for you. Appreciate who she is. Appreciate what she brings to the world. Tell her how wonderful she is. Tell her how beautiful she is. Tell her how much you appreciate her.

Keep it light. Remember how you came together in the first place? Wasn't it delightful? Were you not giddy with excitement to be with that person? Did you not have fun together? Yes, I realize how difficult life can be, how much stress there can be in day-to-day living. It's tiring to raise children, put food on the table, and fulfill all of the other responsibilities and obligations that you have in your marriage, but never lose sight of how and why you came together in the first place. Your mate is your best friend. She was your best friend and companion and playmate when you first met her. Why should that end? Why? Be playmates still. You are devoting your life to this person. This person knows you intimately; you trust her implicitly. So why on earth should you cease to enjoy this person?

So keep things light. Do the things you did in the beginning of the relationship. Lie on a blanket under the stars, late at night, in your backyard. When you are camping, take a canoe out into the middle of the lake under the stars and moon. Put little notes in your loved one's pocket or bag. Pay an unexpected visit to her office and whisk her away for lunch, or any other activity you find exciting. Take mini vacations. You can do this even in your own town or city. Get a babysitter and then go stay at a hotel and sit up watching movies, or go out for dinner, or take a walk around the city. Do the things you would normally not do together. All of these things add up in a real way.

Love each other fiercely. Put each other first. Dote on one another. Respect one another. Be each other's best friend.

I wish I had more time to do these things. There's simply never enough time. I know I will see my darling girl again. I see her all the time as it is. I can love her from afar, which I do. I never really leave her side. I watch over her, protect her, and adore her. There is no distance between her and I; it's a very thin curtain between us.

Love never dies. You take it with you wherever you go. You carry love in your heart. It's eternal. So while I can't physically hold her hand, or kiss her cheek anymore, I am as real as I've ever been and as in love with her as I've ever been. I am with her always. I will never leave her side.

And my children, my beloved children, I feel enormous love and gratitude for these beautiful souls who chose me as their father.

Lisa, are you feeling this love again? It's almost overwhelming. I can hardly contain this much love. Each and every one of them is so precious to me.

Lisa, you're looking at the Radiant Star diamond and you think that it is the most beautiful, brilliant diamond you have ever seen. That is how I feel about these children of mine. Each one of them is a Radiant Star diamond. Each one is unique, brilliant, and special beyond belief. My heart simply overflows with love for these beautiful, cherished children of mine. I watch them, I'm with them, and I'll never let them go.

Can you feel me moving away, Lisa? I am so grateful to you for giving me the chance to tell my loved ones how they fill my heart.

Thank you, thank you, thank you.

Good-bye.

[A few minutes later, I could feel someone around me as I was transcribing the notes. After I finished transcribing, I asked who it was, and it was Paul.]

I just can't pull myself away. It feels like you are my connection to all that I love. Could I come again? I think I'd like to. It's like a telephone line. I feel like I have the connection now and I don't want to cut it off.

My family knew how much I loved them, and yet I feel such a need to express it to them. I feel so sad in this moment because I am unable to get their attention.

I can hear your thoughts, Lisa. You're saying in your mind, "Paul, this all feels very personal and perhaps this should be a private reading at a later date," but this is the way that I want it. It is important for people to know that these bonds of love just continue on for all of eternity. It is important for people to understand that there is no distance between our two worlds. They need to know that I can be as near to her now as I was then—maybe even more so—because I can feel her feelings and hear her thoughts and prayers.

The trouble is that so few people take the time to connect with those in spirit. It can be done. We are all capable of doing that, of making that connection. It can be so healing for those who grieve their loved ones. It really is like picking up a telephone. I would have thought that with all the TV shows out there these days that focus on mediums, it would be all the rage to do so, but there is still some fear and disbelief that keeps people from reaching out to their loved ones.

The one who is overseeing this project, President Lincoln, *he* believed. He knew that connection with Spirit was real. As the New Age community is saying, "The veil is lifting."

I can see you're getting a little restless, Lisa, and tired, and that you anxiously want to call your Robb because it's late. I will not keep you any longer. I will, however, come back, if that's OK?

Lisa: I'm so sorry, Paul. Yes, you're right. I am anxious and restless and tired. It's very late here. I apologize. I know that you have more to say, so by all means, absolutely, please come back. What you have to say is very important. I'm free all day tomorrow so stop by anytime. Thank you for your understanding, Paul. Good night.

Good night.

[I felt bad for "hanging up" on Paul, but I knew that he would be back. If I hadn't been so fidgety and tired, I would have kept the conversation going. I just wasn't in the right space to continue. I felt sure he understood.]

May 5, 2015

[I was transcribing Paul's message while listening to a song called "Chasing Cars" by Snow Patrol. I had the strong sense that someone was around me. I was overcome with feelings of love and sadness. I burst into tears. I was certain that I was taking on someone else's feelings, the feelings of the spirit who was with me. It didn't take long to figure out that Paul was back. He was telling me that the song I was listening to was a message for his wife, that's why I couldn't stop crying. It was beautiful. I felt he was asking his wife to connect with him. I sat quietly and invited him to come in to talk more. The smell of cigarette smoke filled the air.]

Lisa: Paul?

I feel so melancholy at this moment. I feel that if had I taken better care of myself, I might still be with my love. I want to apologize for leaving her. I know she doesn't think these things; it's me thinking them. She just loves me and misses me.

I am sorry I smoked. I am sorry I killed myself with my addiction. I am truly sorry. To you, my darling, I say, *I am sorry.*

She was so lovely. She was so very important to me. She made my life complete. I had a pretty full life, as you can imagine, but it would have been nothing without her. Do you see how important human love is? It's everything, my girl. Everything!

Nothing you acquire, or build, or race, or succeed at can hold a candle to the importance of a loving connection. I am not speaking here of only intimate relationships. I'm speaking of human connections, period.

The bonds that are created and nurtured on Earth are vitally important. There is something so magical about the love that passes from one human being to another. It's shared love. It's fulfillment on the highest human level.

I did try—and succeed at, I must admit—having many shared love bonds. I had that with family, of course, and with friends. Sometimes people came into my life just for a short time, and sometimes they were lifers. That is not important. What IS important is the giving of love. It's bliss.

Now, back to where we left off the other (late) night. It is not only possible to connect with your loved ones on this side of the veil, it is also recommended. It provides comfort for the living and allows the departed to freely move on. When we know that our loved ones can feel us and realize that we are not far away, it comforts us here, and we don't worry. We don't like to see our loved ones suffer. If they understand that they can reach out their hand and it will be held, if they know they can say a prayer and it will be heard, that would comfort them, wouldn't it?

It is that simple, really. All that is required is belief. Believe that love bonds are strong and that they are forever. Believe that we never really die at all. Believe that we simply move to another place for a while.

Pray for your loved ones; they hear you. Talk to them. Have actual conversations with them. They are right there, listening. Share your sadness with them, and your happiness. They are alive and well, just in a different form, a glowing, radiant energy form. It's so beautiful. Know that they watch over you and enjoy you still. No matter how far away they may seem, they are right in front of you, a breath away.

Even as I tell you all of this, I miss my darling girl.

It is hard to be apart, especially when we have been together for such a long time. It's OK to express that sadness because there is also so much love that goes into that sadness. There is a love that will never quit—ever.

I feel I am through here. I came to speak of love and separation. Love is real; separation is not. Believe in love. Know that for all of eternity you will be together with those with whom you have created love bonds. It's very beautiful.

May 15, 2015

[*I was listening to the song "Chasing Cars" again. I suddenly burst into tears, taking on someone's deep feelings of sadness and love. I smelled cigarette smoke strongly and knew it was Paul.*]

The most meaningful thing I did on Earth was love my wife.

I can see that you have fears around loving, Lisa. Please take my advice: love! Remember the lines in your movie: love!

[*He was referencing a scene in the movie Country Strong, in which Gwyneth Paltrow's character is giving Leighton Meester's character some advice on love: "And don't be afraid to fall in love. It's the only thing that matters in life. The only thing. Do you understand what I'm telling you? You just fall in love with as many things as possible."*]

It really IS the most important thing you will ever do. And the best part is the joy you will bring to everyone who comes in contact with you while you are in that love vibration. I know I have to move on, but I am waiting for her. She's not finished down there, but when she is, we will go on together. I know that there are fantastic places here to go to, and I know that I will go because that is the plan, but I am just not prepared to go on without her. I don't mind waiting. Time flies by in this atmosphere. She has lots of living yet to do and I enjoy watching her from here. When it's time, we will journey together, just like we did down there.

It feels a little sad, talking to her this way, and yet, at the same time, it is so wonderful that I can't stop smiling. What a gift to me! And if my words can help others in any way, well then, that's terrific. It's like love, Lisa; you give love because it's what your soul needs for itself, yet it ends up fulfilling and healing others. That is how I feel about this. I came in to speak to my beautiful wife, to send my love to her, and my words might just end up fulfilling and healing perfect strangers. It's a grand design, isn't it?

So remember those words: "Don't be afraid to fall in love. It's the only thing that matters in life. The only thing."

It's really the most important thing I have to say. I hope my contribution to this project helps.

Thank you for bringing me to her.

ENDNOTES:

Paul Newman had one of Hollywood's most legendary marriages and was well known for his devotion to his wife and family. When asked about infidelity, he famously said, "Why go out for a hamburger when you have steak at home?"

Paul Newman's wedding vows are reported to have been:

Happiness in marriage is not something that just happens. A good marriage must be created. In the Art of Marriage, the little things are the big things. It is never being too old to hold hands. It is remembering to say "I love you" at least once a day. It is never going to sleep angry.

It is at no time taking the other for granted; the courtship should not end with the honeymoon; it should continue through all the years. It is having a mutual sense of values and common objectives. It is standing together facing the world. It is forming a circle of love that gathers in the whole family. It is doing things for each other, not in the attitude of duty or sacrifice, but in the spirit of joy.

It is speaking words of appreciation and demonstrating gratitude in thoughtful ways. It is not expecting the husband to wear a halo or the wife to have wings of an angel. It is not looking for perfection in each other.

It is cultivating flexibility, patience, understanding, and a sense of humor. It is having the capacity to forgive and forget. It is giving each other an atmosphere in which each can grow. It is finding room for the things of the spirit. It is a common search for the good and the beautiful.

It is establishing a relationship in which the independence is equal, dependence is mutual, and the obligation is reciprocal. It is not only marrying the right partner; it is being the right partner.

Cleopatra

May 3, 2015 — *Take Back Your Power*

*[I found myself adjusting my posture so that I was sitting perfectly erect.
I suddenly felt noble and important.]*

I have been asleep for a very long time, although it's not called
"sleep" over here; it's more of a rest, a time to gather up all of the soul
fragments of oneself. I have been scattered about, having different
experiences at the same time, bringing them all together, integrating
them, coalescing and then familiarizing myself with these parts that I
have been away from for a while—a long while.

Then there is the process of review. This gives all the parts a chance
to see what the others have been up to. We have all had different
lifetimes, sometimes at the same time, and we come together to
integrate the knowledge and experiences that we have had.

This took me a long time in Earth years. There were a lot of parts, a lot of lifetimes, and a lot of experiences. There was so much to go over, to reminisce about, to discuss.

As Cleopatra, I had what you would call a very important lifetime. That was not an easy role that I played. It required much of me. So many times, I wanted to run away with my lover, to focus only on love and lust. To be ordinary, a woman in love. My heart was always called in that direction. And sometimes I had to go, and so I did. And when I did so, it breathed new life into me. It gave me what I needed to continue on in my role as Cleopatra, the ruler.

Are you surprised that I call myself a "ruler"? You should not be. Throughout history, women have been—sometimes silently, sometimes obviously—rulers, in charge. We have ruled from the throne; from behind the curtain; from inside the home; and out in the community, the villages, and the world at large.

Women give life. They nurture life. You could say, women create life. Woman protect life. It is within us, on the very deepest level, to do that. This creates an environment for more life to flow. That is why women leaders are a wonderful gift to the world.

I ruled in that time, in that era, just as if I had sat on the throne myself. I was respected by most—revered, even, at times. There were also those who wanted me gone. I was always alert to those who would do me wrong. I protected myself and I had many protecting me, as well.

But much of my life was spent with people, and before people, who honored and respected me. I stood straight and tall, as every woman should. We are the bearers of fruit, the bearers of life. We have so much collective wisdom as women, so much connectivity to All That Is, that if we were to band together, this world would be changed in an instant!

I call to the women! Gather your sisters and stand together. Unite as one. Form circles in your homes and in your neighborhoods and in your cities. Let that circle widen out into the world. It is so easy in your generation to make those connections, even with people on the other side of the world.

I urge you, women of this world, come together as one! When you come together as one, as one heart, as one life, the men will bow before you.

Your world needs help. The ground and all that grows from it is crying out to be healed. Mother Earth herself is waiting for you to step back into your power, as women, as the giver of life itself, to say, "No more death! No more death!"

The world is dying. She's dying. So many lives on your planet are lost every day through war, abuse, poverty. As women in charge, we would never let this happen. NEVER. We would be protecting all the young, as do herds in the animal kingdom. We would do whatever it took to restore life to that which is decayed and dying.

Do you realize, women, how much power you hold in your hands and in your hearts and in your minds? Enough to completely restore this world back to its wholeness!

Lisa, can you feel the power surging through you?

Lisa: Yes.

That is the feeling of power. Genuine, authentic power that comes from the Divine itself. Breathe in life! Feel your strong bodies! Stand tall and firm! Take back your power, women!

I say this: If you began today to do this thing, your hearts would overflow with love. You would dance in celebration of what you could accomplish.

The full moon that appears on this day was once honored by the Feminine Goddess. Understand the power of the moon, and the tides, and the Earth, and the rhythms and cycles of the Earth, and your bodies.

When your circles come together, stand under the full moon as often as you can. Hold hands and pray for this power to continue to fill you up so that you can march on! And then dance a dance of gratitude that it has been done!

In every country across the land, this can be done. Start in your own neighborhood, with your own coworkers, family, and groups.

Start with words. Talk about this power that is inside of you. Talk about the life that comes through you. Talk about the vision that you hold for the world. Inspire each other. Elevate each other. Love each other.

In the beginning was the word. Speak the word! It's time, women!

I will lead you forward in this march of love. Call on the Divine Creator to give you strength, wisdom, courage, faith, and the will to change the world. There is a saying, "Never doubt that a small group of thoughtful, committed people can change the world. Indeed, it is the only thing that ever has."

Stand up straight and tall, women, and fight for life. Fight for peace. Fight for equality. Fight for dignity. Fight for love.

We on the other side of the veil will support you and uplift you.

Stand in your own truth. Stand in your own power. It is Divine.

Davy Jones

May 6, 2015 — *I'm a Believer!*

[*I could feel someone come in. While I was waiting to see who it was, I couldn't help smiling; I couldn't contain the feeling of joy. I was feeling excited, like I was about to meet up with a long-lost friend. It was Davy Jones!*]

Lisa: Well, it's about time! Were you avoiding me, so you didn't have to hear "I told you so"?

First of all, I love the song you play to get you in the zone! [*"My Sweet Lord" by George Harrison*] It's just such a great, happy song. It makes me wanna dance! Let's just finish the song before we continue, shall we?

Oh, man! YOU WERE RIGHT! There, I said it! Do you feel better?

Lisa: Ha-ha! I'm just happy to hear from you. I really wondered if you would come through. I looked at a photo of us recently. It's the photo that someone took of us while we were discussing life after death.

It's my pleasure. Really, Lisa, this is a trip! I came over here and, I have to admit, I was a little lost. Maybe *confused* is a better word. *Disoriented* might even be better. No, *confused.* I didn't quite know what to make of my experience. It was not what I expected! But secretly, I can tell you now, it's what I was hoping for.

I mean, think about it. If you go through life believing that "when you're dead, you're dead," well, that makes you sure wanna have a great and full life—live every moment like it's your last. But it's just a little bit scary as you get older. The idea of not existing anymore is just not one that puts a smile on your face, that's for sure.

So it's true that I didn't believe in anything after death, but it's one time that I WANTED to be wrong. And so I am!

This place is unbelievable! Anything and everything! Whatever earthly pleasures and enjoyments you want to have more of, you can. If it's your favorite food, no problem. If it's music, it's here. Get-togethers with friends, those too. If it's rest you seek, it's a perfect place for that.

What's so neat is that it's all here, but surprisingly, it's not chaotic. It just kind of IS. You just tell them what you want, and they get it for you. Now, don't ask me who "they" are. I haven't figured out all of that yet. They feel like benevolent beings, like angels or something. Oh, man, listen to me!

This place is almost magical. The air is velvety, smooth, almost fluid. It's so hard to put into words that you would understand down there. There's nothing like it where you are right now.

It's soft air, gentle. Soft like a kitten. Everything is just so sweet. Melodic. With the most vibrant colors I have ever seen. There's nothing to compare it to at all on Earth, just no basis of comparison. I'm sorry; I'm trying. But remember, I'm still just trying to take this all in. I didn't expect anything!

People (do I call them that?) are constantly moving here; floating is more like it. Just whooshing by, here and there, but with a purpose, an intention. Now, don't mistake that to mean driven, and fast-paced and hectic like it can be down there. No, these beings are all moving, but the essence of everything they do is so smooth. That's the best way I can describe it. Smooth, yeah, like smooth jazz.

And speaking of music, oh my! The music here is outta this world! It's an octave and pitch that is not present in your realm. It is truly what I would've imagined angels would sound like if they were singing—if I believed in angels, say!

I'm strolling by a stream right now. Just brushing my hand through the water as I walk by. Again, smooth. The water feels smooth. Everything feels smooth. It's indescribable, really, the feeling here. I've never felt peace like this down there. It wouldn't be possible. I'm not sure what is going to happen, where I will go next, what it's like in other places up here, but there is just a sense of total trust in the process here. There is no need to know things here. No need to control anything or worry about anything. All that is just wasted space and time. It doesn't belong here.

I haven't had time to think too much about what is going on down there. I've been so caught up in this incredible journey. This incredible, unexpected journey. I do think about my children, though. I'm thinking of them right now. I'd like to tell them I'm all right. Really, all right. REALLY, REALLY all right—better than ever! I don't think I've ever felt so good or so alive! Wow!

And my youngest, she thinks of me so much, and misses me. I hear you, baby girl. Just know daddy's having a really nice time around here. I'm loving this! I see you and feel deep gratitude for all of you in my life. Pride and gratitude are what I'm feeling. You are beautiful children and you are beautiful souls. I can see your souls from up here. They are so lovely. Can you believe I am saying these things? Trippy, right? Huh!

Aside from my children, I am happy to be here. I enjoyed living—don't get me wrong—it was one hell of a life! But this, this is something else! My message has to be that there IS something else afterward. I'm living proof—ha-ha! Ah, I can't help it! Everyone knew I loved to joke. And that's the neat thing here: I'm the same as I was—at least, I think so. I haven't been here long enough to know what's what, but so far, I feel like the same Davy that left your place, just more peaceful. Restful. Calm. Happy. Centered. Fulfilled. Complete. It's really quite a nice surprise.

[*His energy made me feel so full of joy, like I wanted to burst into a giggle the whole time. It was playful, happy energy. What a great feeling!*]

Lisa, there is so much to tell you. I could go on and on. Can I go on and on? How much time do you have?

Lisa: Lots.

OK, then I will.

It's a dreamy state of existence here, ethereal, unlike anything I could have imagined. Everyone has an energy about him or her. Instead of names, we know each other by our various energies. Every single person has a different energy, like fingerprints, I suppose. It's amazing. You can pick up what people are thinking and feeling all the time. It's so transparent here. Can you imagine what that would be like on Earth? Everyone knowing what everyone was thinking and feeling? Well, that could be a good thing—or not! It's refreshing, though, just being so open with everyone. It's comfortable.

There are only welcoming, loving supportive interactions here. Gone completely is harshness or any strong negative emotions. There is just no place here for that. It's a place for rejuvenation, regeneration, relaxation, and reunion. The four R's. There are more R's if you want: rest, renewal, rebirth, and renunciation. And remembering—remembering what we are all made of, what we are all made for, what we are all doing with each other.

There is still a lot I have not learned here, but I can say that even in this short time, I know that what we believe to be important down there means nada up here. There is simply no inclination here to be anything but happy and at peace. To unite with others, to support others, to care for and enjoy others. It's such a nice change from how it all goes down, down there.

I hope people take a page out of this book and start to practice now what they will soon live. I think I did a pretty good job down there, in a lot of areas, but there were other areas where I failed. Maybe "failed" is too strong a word. "Missed the mark" is a better way to say it.

Lisa: Davy, can we pick this up again tomorrow? It's getting late here, I'm tired, and I have a headache.

Of course. Just give me a shout tomorrow then. This has been swell so far! Good night.

Lisa: Good night Davy, it's been interesting and fun talking to you. Your energy is so light and fresh and happy and silly, actually. What a treat! I can't stop smiling, even with the headache! Thanks!

May 17, 2015

[*I felt happy and silly inside again. I knew it was Davy coming back!*]

Oh, man! It's good to be back! It IS so great here, believe me, but it's also nice joining you there and sharing my stories.

Let's see, where was I . . . telling my tales from behind the veil. Yes, that WOULD be a good title for the book; I know that is what you just thought! Not so much *tales*, but familiarizing you with what's over here. Hmmm . . . where to go next?

I'm still being playful here, just like there. We are more or less the same here as we were there. Of course, there is growth and awareness that occurs here, so one doesn't stay the same, but that takes some time. It's not like we just—poof!—become someone else. Nope, it's a process, like everything else, it seems.

So I remain playful. I hope that stays with me because I love that side of me. Not taking things too seriously is a good thing, I think, there or here. What's the point? What's to get all serious about, just to find that what we took so seriously and fretted about vanishes into thin air? It seems kind of silly, doesn't it? Kind of a waste of energy, huh?

Try to float through life being as carefree and relaxed as you can, like your best friend, Lori, does. Just float through life. Easy. That's a good word: easy. Be easy. What a difference it makes to those around you when you do that, not to mention, to your health and life in general. Remember to be easy.

That's what it's all about here, floating through the days without a care in the world. There is no specific schedule for anything. No schedule to learn, to relax, to plan. The time for everything is just when it feels right. What a way to live, hey?

I like keeping it light, always have. It makes things so much more enjoyable. Even the so-called important stuff can be made so much better with a light touch. When you realize that nothing lasts but love anyway, why be so concerned with the other things? Why be concerned with what to *do* with other things, how to *keep* other things—even your health, or relationships, and for sure, material things? There's no need to cling, that's for sure. There's no need to fear change or loss of anything. It's just not worth your consideration, never mind your energy or focus. Just allow them to float on out of your life if that is what is happening. And be open to seeing the new things that will appear in their place. Believe me, if you let the things that are ready to go, go, remarkable new things will take their place— whether they're actual things, or experiences, or people. Don't hang on to what is ready to go. It just serves no purpose.

That is what we are so concerned with on Earth, keeping things, holding on tightly to things. It seems silly from up here because those things just dissolve into nothingness when you let them. It's time to move on then.

Everyone's happy here. What's not to be happy about? It's like Christmas morning, Las Vegas, love, and vacations all rolled into one—all the time! People need to let their fear of death go! There is absolutely no need to be afraid. You will experience the most profound joy, peace, and love here, with no downside. There is no need to fear losing any of it, ever! There is just nowhere for it to go. It just IS here.

If people could wrap their minds around this truth, that they are more fully alive here than there, wow! Would they ever be afraid?

I am so grateful for this opportunity to pop in and share my new reality with all of you reading this.

Keep it light, people. Keep it silly. Keep it positive. Hold onto things loosely. Relax. Play. That's what I have to say.

I might be done here.

ENDNOTES:

In 2008, I met Davy and his band after a performance in Calgary. My friends and I hung out with them for the evening. Davy and I somehow got on the topic of spirituality, particularly the question of whether the soul survives death. He didn't believe so, saying, "When you're dead, you're dead, Lisa." I replied, "Davy, let me schedule you for a past-life regression and let's see what happens."

Here are two photos taken of us, one while he and I were deep in the discussion about life after death. He was such a happy guy, and really nice. What an enjoyable evening I had.

Jesus

May 10, 2015 — *Perfect and Beautiful*

[*I was feeling so much love in my heart that I began to cry. The first thing I saw was George Harrison wearing white, standing incredibly straight and tall and at peace. He looked like a Master. My heart was filled with love, looking at him. It was as if Jesus were standing there. I felt at peace. He appeared the way I would expect a Master to, like Jesus. It was somewhat confusing to me. Then he faded into the background, it seemed, and Jesus actually came forth.*]

I will go before all the guests. I will lead them in from now on. I will bring them in white Light.

Lisa, why do you weep?

Lisa: You are so beautiful. Your light is so bright. I feel like I did before, wanting to say, "Why me? I am not worthy of this job."

[Tears were streaming down my face.]

What did I ask you all those years ago? I asked, "What are you?" And you answered?

Lisa: Perfect and beautiful.

This is the time that you will finally be able to tell the world what I showed you that day. I showed you that all people are made in the image and likeness of the Father. There is nothing but perfect beauty in everyone—nothing but a perfect form housing a perfect God. You think that you are here to work and to advance yourselves. That is not why any of you are here. You are here simply to grow in love. If you did nothing but love, you would accomplish everything.

That realm, that vibration that you are living and working in, is so harsh. It is so difficult for you to see yourselves clearly there. It's like being thrown in mud. You are all covered in it. You like that reference, don't you? Only when you are washed clean of all that is not you, do you see yourselves as you truly are.

When I lived on Earth, it was so difficult to stay close to my Father while in Earth's heavy energy. Oh, to be constantly steeped in the mud of Earth, the forgetfulness, the negativity, the heaviness, the dark emotions. Many times, I fell. I forgot who I was and why I had come. I had a mission, so I had many Masters come to remind me and to pick me up.

You all pray for help. Please know that help is there. It is always with you. It comes in the form of angels. Angels surround you all. There are so many spirit beings around each and every one of you that if you could see them, you would never feel alone. You are never alone. Your loved ones are with you. Your angels and guides are around you.

Take their hand and let them pick you up.

Lisa, I asked you so long ago to tell the world what I had shown you. Now is your chance. Tell them. It is important that they know that they are loved and cared for always, not only when they behave in ways that please. *Always*. They need to know that they have been created as perfect reflections of God. People need to know that despite what they have done, or ever will do, they are perfect in the eyes of God. Nothing that any of you do is judged as less than perfect. Tell them, Lisa, what I showed you that day.

Lisa, is there any more important message to share? If this book only said that one thing, "You are perfect and beautiful," it would be complete, but people are not ready to hear that. They want to hold onto the distortion that they are bad and flawed and wrong and separate and unworthy. That is a big one: unworthy. You struggle with this most of all, as do so many.

To each one of you I say: You are a magnificent being. You are God incarnate, filled with everything in the universe. You are here to love. You are fully alive, with so much Light that you could illuminate the entire world if only you would allow it to come to the surface to be seen.

You are mighty and powerful, lowly and meek. You are in this world but not of it. You are the one for whom you have truly been waiting. The search is over; you are here. All that is needed is for you to believe in who you are, in what you are.

Each of you is an extension of God, and each other. What you see outside of yourself IS yourself. Do not be fooled into thinking that there is anything besides yourself. There is not. Each of the parts of yourself are being acted out in the lives of others. You are the sum total of everyone who ever lived. What you do not live and experience, your brother will, so that God can have a full experience of Himself. I will use "Him," but you know we are beyond gender.

When you look at another and judge him as less than, as inferior, as lowly, that is simply you that you judge. He is simply a part of you—a beautiful part of you. When you look at another and praise him for being great and wonderful, strong and good, that is also you that you praise—another beautiful part of you.

You cannot have one without the other. It is impossible. These two sides are necessary for the whole to be whole. And you are nothing if not whole. So the brokenness you observe in others, the meanness you judge in others, the stinginess you dislike in others, the brilliance you praise in others, the light you see in others—all of it is you. Do you understand that? Until you understand this concept, you will not move on.

They are parts of your very self. Love all parts of yourself as they are reflected in others. Embrace all aspects of yourself completely. Forgive all actions of others promptly. Love all of yourself deeply and holistically.

Lisa, your body is tired, so I will step away from you now. I am never far away, so you will feel me. I will come to speak with you more, as this is the time for people to wake up and live as God.

Albert Einstein

May 16, 2015 — *The Theory of Irrelevance*

This is very different for me. I didn't know this was possible, unlike Lincoln. I am fascinated by this process. It's truly remarkable.

Forgive my timidity. I am somewhat hesitant to step forward and yet I know it will be as important as anything else I did on Earth.

When I was there, I was revered for my intellect, but not always. I struggled in childhood and was ridiculed. Then, when I proved myself, I was celebrated and admired. I can see from this vantage point that neither should be believed. What people think of you there is of no consequence. You see, they will praise or condemn as they see fit, as the fashion is, as their perception is, as their evolutionary level dictates.

All of it is just opinion, judgment, and perception. Nothing of another's view of you is real. Do not, under any circumstance, let your fellow man judge you, even favorably. It means absolutely nothing, as he or she could in an instant adopt an unfavorable judgment. Do you see how this just keeps you bouncing from favor to disfavor? It puts so much power in another's hands, where it does not belong.

The only judge of you is YOURSELF, and even that is not reliable. It is not reliable because it is not based on truth, but rather, on conditioning and patterns of belief from this and other lifetimes that you carry inside of you. Again, it's not the truth, just perception. When I came over here, I thought I was really something. I thought I was very important. That didn't last long, however. I learned very quickly that the measure of a man's worth is not based on accomplishments and achievements in any area of his life. We are all worthy, infinitely so. There is only Divine perfection in all of us and once we arrive on this side of the veil, we see that; it's the great equalizer. I mean GREAT! Can you accept, you down there, that all men are, in fact, equal? Can you accept that, whether a man is a janitor or a great inventor, he is the exact same: valuable beyond measure!

This is true. It's something I learned here and the idea of it fills me with a love that is inexpressible. No one is any more special than another. No one's life is more important. No one is worthy of more praise or admiration than another.

All that is required is for you to live your life fully and in integrity with YOUR soul purpose, no matter what that is. It is for no one else to judge because he or she cannot know your soul's path.

So if you are someone who struggles with being admired, respected, and supported, now is the time to stop seeking that and realize that you are absolutely everything right and beautiful, now. If you are a person who is being admired, respected, and supported for what others deem to be worthy, now is the time to stop allowing that to feed you falsely. Know your worth in every instance. You are worthy simply because *you are*. No achievement, accomplishment, money, or success can give you that, or more of that; it's who you are. If you go through this life with no earthly "notable" achievement, be clear that you are still a high and holy being.

In every case, whether your life is judged as small and insignificant or noble and accomplished, you are infinitely worthy, whole, and perfect. Shake off the desire—no, the need—for this world's judgment. Just walk your path, live your life, and know that no one can assign you worth. It's yours forever.

That was the realization I had when I arrived here. I had such a false sense of myself, of my importance. I had to be shown, very carefully, how to take all those ego layers off of myself and reside in the place of truth. The truth about myself was far more powerful and grand than any I could have concocted on my own. To learn that nothing assigned to me by the world in my Earth lives had any value, but that the core of me, the essence of me, was so incredibly magnificent and valuable, was a great surprise.

That is my message to you: value yourself now, right now, the way that you are, for who you are—not for any other reason, except that you ARE. In this way, you will not be blown here and there by the winds and whims of others; rather, you will be solid within yourself, able to focus on simply the action of living.

I am so happy to have learned this finally. I now feel like an advanced soul, one who can share my discovery with others. Even the term "advanced" is meaningless and a judgment, but I will use it to distinguish myself now from what I thought of as being advanced while on Earth. I hope you understand my meaning.

I thank you for your time, and for allowing me to share this important message. I hope it helps in some way.

Good day.

George Harrison

May 17, 2015 — *No Wrong Choices*

[*I felt like crying as I played the song, "My Sweet Lord," to set the vibration of the session.*]

I am so happy that you are writing this in such a way as to touch on the things that are important rather than the things that merely entertain.

I am behind this work. I feel privileged to be part of it. It's what I tried so hard to focus on in my life. But as you know, life does get in the way.

First of all, thank you so much for using my song to set the vibration of each session. I can see how much the song moves you. It was written because I had such devotion to my God, as do you, so I can appreciate your experience in listening to it.

Lisa, in a parallel universe I could have seen myself as a wanderer, seeker, mystic. There were so many times that I wished I were not famous so that I could have pursued my heart's journey: that of enlightenment. I can see now, from this vantage point, that all was as it should have been. John was right about something important: we do choose our path, long before we arrive on Earth. Throughout life we may not understand why a certain thing is happening, but that is not important. What is important is that we know that we do choose it.

My happiest moments in life, besides being with my family, were being with my God. I often felt like I was born in the wrong era, like I should have been born in a time and place that would have respected my search for God and my deep desire to connect with the Divine, while in a human body. But there's no time for dreaming of things that were not to be. I can always have that experience next, should I want to.

I was very well loved in my lifetime by my wives, my son, my family, my friends, my fans. I had everything, materially, as well. I was a blessed man in life—very, very blessed. I appreciated most of it, most of the time. Not always, of course. I WAS human, after all.

If I could do it over again, I would have done it just the same way. I say that because it really was perfect—my life and my choices—as are everyone's. There is no need to "do over" because each experience is just that: an experience! No more, no less.

I have only one message to share and that is to be present in your experience. Show up. Stop believing that if this were different or that were different, that your life would be right or perfect. It is right, right now. And certainly do not look back on anything in the past, things done that perhaps you are not happy with, and think that those choices were somehow wrong. Nothing you chose could be wrong. It is just a merry-go-round existence. Round and round, we try on all kinds of lives, round and round. We have experiences that add to our soul's collective whole. From all of it, we become and embody the wholeness that we seek.

It is a miracle, life. It is a gift. I often, like you, wished I could have escaped it, thinking that the real truth lay on the other side of the veil, and it does, but living the Earth life, again and again, is where the richness lies. When you live enough times, and gather enough experiences, then you bring the truth from this side, there. Does that make sense?

Lisa: Yes.

So really value your time there and treat it as a precious gift. Do not judge any of your choices in life as bad, or a waste of time; they are absolutely not! Each one is exactly right for you and your soul's evolution. That is something I was surprised to learn here. And if my sharing this can help people to live more fully, with less angst and guilt and remorse, then I am happy.

All paths DO lead to the same place: wholeness. We walk along this Earth journey with each other as companions. We are all trying hard to get it right when we are there. The funny thing is, we are always right. There is nothing else but rightness.

I am enjoying my peace here—sheer peace. It is heavenly. There is nothing I feel to do, except just sink into it and stay in it for as long as I wish. I don't concern myself with what is next for me. It's enough to BE. That's how it's done here. And it is deeply satisfying.

[I was listening to his song and feeling like crying.]

Lisa, I feel that I am really connecting with you. We have a similar vibration and essence. At least as I had when I was there. We would have felt a complete resonance with one another had we met and we could have been great friends, learning from one another, spending much of our time in the pursuit of enlightenment. We would have spoken the same language, you might say.

That is why it is such a treat to speak to you now. Just as I preferred spiritual discussion there, I prefer it here now. You care about my spiritual journey and I appreciate that more than you know.

Just so you know, we are all going to get there. It's the place we are going and nothing can stop it. So don't worry about how long it seems to be taking to get there; just be comforted knowing that you *are* getting there. You will understand this. I say it because you worry about this. There really is no need to. You are right where you need to be. Frustrating to hear this, isn't it? But I can see now that it is true for all of us.

I have to say again, Lisa, I, for one, am so pleased that this book is focusing on what is important in life. I am happy that that is the way it has been designed from this side. It's a complete match for me and what my intentions and desires would have been for a book. The fact that the vibration in my song helps you in the process, well, that is just marvelous! You honor me with that.

I will step back now into my peaceful paradise. It's been a unique and special visit. I support this work 1,000 percent!

Blessings from near and far.

Paul Gauguin

May 19, 2015 — *Life Is Art*

What a mystery this is. It's a mystery to me because I didn't know this was possible, at least, not in the time I lived. Now I believe anything.

This is incredible. How positively wonderful it is to be able to communicate this way.

Oh my, I am just going over in my mind what I would like to say. I feel I have so many things that I could talk about, but I don't want to get carried away and usurp all the time.

Well, first of all, I am so pleased to be here, pleased and delighted. I wish to start off by saying, "Come on, everyone, when you can see how easy this is to do, how possible it is, how could you ever mourn anyone?" It's a little like when someone in your life moves to another geographic location. You don't get to see him anymore, but you can pick up a telephone and connect with him easily and often. When you speak to him it feels like he is right with you, doesn't it? Well, this is the same thing. I am from another era entirely and voilà! Here I am! It's so simple. It's magical, almost. It's very easy.

I encourage everyone reading this to pick up the phone! Dial someone you love. It's as easy as one-two-three! No more tears and sadness. Yes, you can still miss your loved one's physical presence, but you should not be separated from them again, not ever, really.

This just feels so good! I feel almost alive! This is the way I felt when I painted—alive! It was what I lived for! If I could have done it all day and night, I would have. It brought me the utmost pleasure and satisfaction.

That is the way it is supposed to be, you know. All of you should be doing what brings you the aliveness that you seek. Some of you do some of the things that bring some aliveness and pleasure to you, some of the time. Do you follow me? *Some*. But most of you do none of the things that bring you to the place of aliveness and pleasure, most of the time.

This life that you are living is for exactly that: life! How can you live life, be alive in life, when you live mostly in a dead zone? I don't want to lecture anyone here so I will try to keep this light. But come on, people, open yourselves up to really living!

Let me ask you, why do you work at things that keep you feeling apathetic, bored, and dead inside? Because that is all you think you can do? Because your family or society said you should? Because you are too afraid to dream bigger than that? Oh, I am sure there are more reasons you could come up with to answer that question, but none of them would be good ones.

I am telling you this: it is not supposed to be this way. You were not put on the planet to toil and slave at things that cause you to die. That is not living, you see, that is dying. You are dying slow, boring deaths!

Strike out! Set sail in a new direction! It is NEVER too late for you to do this. I am speaking here to those who think they are too old. You can do it. You would be wise to do so, even at this juncture of your life.

But to the young people, I say with such passion, strike out! Go down your OWN path! Go down the path that you are excited to go down. Find your own unique path and follow it. Do not allow anyone to choose that path for you— not parents, not friends, not teachers. Do not look to society for the truth and the way. Silence the voice of fear within you; it lies to you.

Be brave, all of you, and truly start living your lives! I urge you to heed my words. If I had done so, if I had spent all of my years living my passion, I may have lived many years longer. You see, when you are alive with passion and fulfilled in that, you can override biology— what the world thinks of biology. Joy and an unlimited spirit are the keys to longevity. Dreaming and moving toward those dreams keeps you young, and a young and happy spirit can keep you going forever!

So, please, people—especially you sparkly young people— love yourselves enough to confidently move toward what you authentically want to do. When you do that, the whole world will support you. You will attract what you need and the circumstances of your journey will align with great precision to bring you to the place you envision for yourselves. All you need is a willing spirit and plenty of courage. You will need courage because I can see that not much has changed since I was around; there just isn't much support for doing your own thing, is there?

There is so much pressure on the young to conform, yet they house within themselves the full knowledge of not only their own destiny and truth, but also, the planet's. Every one of you knows deep down how it's supposed to be. I don't know how humans got off on the wrong foot, the foot that says there is only one way to do things. From what I can see, that is just not true.

Again, this is not a lecture. God knows how much I limited myself—such a shame. I was in heaven (just like now) when I painted! Can you imagine how my life would have looked had I stayed perpetually in that heavenly state? How my health would have been? How my relationships would have been? Bliss, I tell you, pure bliss.

I was going to speak to the artists out there, specifically, but how are they separate from the rest? All of life is art! Whether you run your own business or care for others, whether you play a sport or a piano, it's all just art—and that is what I speak to. Let yourselves off the death hook! Let yourselves experience true life, then just watch and see how your lives transform before your very eyes. It will be startling!

Whatever keeps you feeling dead inside, toss it out; just change direction. Change whatever you need to in order to give yourselves the gift of life.

I can see that I am starting to repeat myself here, so I will stop. It's just that I am so passionate about passion.

In the beginning, I was supported by my loved ones in my artistic endeavors. I was the one who betrayed myself with my ideas of how much time to allot for my art. What a shame. Life is a grand adventure—at least it ought to be; really drink from the cup of life! There will be plenty of time to rest when you get over to where I am. The interesting thing is that as soon as you get here, you will want to go back and do it again—like an amusement park ride! You have an opportunity down there that you signed up for, a great one at that, so don't waste a moment doing anything that does not feel in total alignment with your soul's joy.

OK, off my soapbox now.

Hmmm . . . what else can I say from up here? Well, another thing that is important, at least as I see it, is how you value yourselves and your gifts. Every single person is valuable and gifted. Every one of you reading this is. Do you believe me?

Do not think that because you can't paint, you are not gifted. Your life and all that you do and how you do it is a gift. How you speak to others is a gift. How you bring a smile to someone's face is a gift. How you wrap a present, in your own unique way, is a gift. How you fix a meal, or your car, is a gift. How you arrange furniture or tell a story is a unique gift. All of it is a gift, and so valuable to the world. You are a gift, as is your very life.

Your world could not be what it is without your presence in it. You are as important as the president, as the pop star, as the doctor, as the scientist, as the artist. All of you bring your uniqueness to the mix and you are all highly valuable to the whole. Your world just would not BE without you. Can you grasp that concept? Please let that sink in. It would not BE without you!!

Do you feel important now? You should! You are unquestionably necessary for this world to be. Quite a notion, isn't it?

Please take the time to honor yourselves and your contribution to the whole. Honor your gifts and talents, your personality, your strengths, and your participation. Spend time with yourselves in self-reflection and affirmation. Treat yourselves well. Celebrate yourselves often, for some reason, or for no reason at all. Believe that you are beautiful and important and grand because you are, each one of you. You are far more valuable than any priceless gemstone or work of art. You are as important as oxygen to the planet. You are as mighty as God. Celebrate it all!

If you have children, help them to feel their importance. Tell your children how special they are and help them to see themselves that way. Teach them how to show others their own worth. What a gift you give them when you do this. That's parenting at its finest!

I lived in a time when it was difficult to focus on the self. It was a heavy and dark time. There was no room then for this self-reflection and celebration. It would have seemed absurd to speak of these things during that time in history. Life was much harder and people were closed.

These times that you are living in are ideal for this outfoldment. Yes, to fold out. To blossom. To bloom. To open. To explode into Light— and right. It's the right time to know yourselves, value yourselves, celebrate yourselves and share yourselves—YOURselves—with the world!

Au revoir, special ones.

ENDNOTES:

"No one is good; no one is evil; everyone is both, in the same way and in different ways. ... It is so small a thing, the life of a man, and yet there is time to do great things, fragments of the common task."
—Paul Gauguin, Intimate Journals, 1903

In 1871, Gauguin worked as a stockbroker in Paris at the age of twenty-three. In 1879 he was earning 30,000 francs a year (about $125,000) as a stockbroker, and as much again in his dealings in art. In 1882 the Paris stock market crashed and the art market dried up. His earnings dropped sharply and he decided to pursue painting full time. Gauguin's life had many ups and downs, including dismissive reviews and extreme financial struggles, and he was vastly underappreciated during his life, but he left us with great works of art.

Martin Luther King Jr.

May 21, 2015 — In You, It Is Done

I am considered a Master soul because of the work I did and my overriding intention to elevate humanity. I don't see myself that way at all. I simply want what we all do, deep inside. The only difference between me and some others is that I had the courage to act on my heart.

It takes great courage to go against the norm and stand up for what feels right deep in our souls. It takes great courage. Who among you has this? Anyone who has, step forth and join the cause. What is the cause? Justice. Equality. Freedom.

There is still so much oppression in your world. It's not so much in the first worlds—yet even there, it is present—but it exists in all other parts of the world. Why is this so? Why are people suffering anywhere? Why, I ask?

Do to others what you would have done to yourselves. Would you wish for a family member to be persecuted, abused, or starved? Do you think those on the other side of the world are any different than your very own flesh and blood? They are not. You ARE them, simply in different skin. Feel deep into yourself and you will know I speak the truth here. Not one of you deserves to be treated less than another. It is criminal for this to occur. When you give to your charities, it is good. It carries the vibration of love. But when you stand up for another, when you defend their rights, you are closer to the truth of your being. Those people near you and on the other side of the planet are your brothers and sisters. More than that, they are you. So roll up your sleeves and go to work for them. Walk alongside them. Speak for them if they have no voice. Support them. Love them. That effort is an even higher vibration of love.

If a person goes to church on Sunday and sings and prays and dances, and then leaves the building carrying with him or her the same judgment and prejudices, he or she may as well have slept in that morning.

It is not good enough to pretend to be a servant of God. It is not good enough to say the prayers and then forget them one hour later. Live it! Embrace it with all your heart and mind and soul!

I speak now to the young. As I look down on the Earth and what is happening there, I see a very beautiful thing. I see a whole youth contingency with an elevated consciousness, just waiting to express itself. Do you realize how powerful all of you are? Do you realize that you have the power to completely shift the energy of the Earth? Do you?

You have come in, many of you, with a mission, a purpose beyond yourselves. You have an awareness, an understanding of how things work, that is far greater than your parents have. You carry the seed of the enlightened era that is ahead of you. You have purposely chosen to incarnate at this time of great change. YOU are the change-makers!

If you think that what I did was great, oh, you just wait and see what you will do! You have more intention as a whole group than I ever had. You carry the blueprint of the new Earth within you.

It makes the transcriber here feel overwhelmed with love. She can feel the power and force of love within you as a group.

Even in the second and third worlds, as they are called there, the youth have come in remembering their divine heritage. They want to break away from what their parents and teachers and society have taught them. It does not fit into their higher reality and their knowing hearts. They envision a world that is unified and ONE. That is their destiny, to bring this vision that they carry in their hearts and minds into reality on Earth.

It's like the hippies of my generation, but with a clearer vision and greater resolve to see the changes through to the end. You young people do not want separation, war, prejudice, discrimination, or any other kind of lower vibrational energy manifestations on the planet. You want a simpler life with more love, equality, unity, and peace. You young people carry such a strong world vision of Oneness that it will come to pass.

You beautiful young souls, keep connecting with one another through your social media. Connect with those on the other side of the world. Those of you who are meant to be leaders, step out and speak up. Speak for and against. For love and equality, for Oneness and peace. And speak against bigotry, separation, prejudice, and persecution in all their forms.

I will lend my strength to you, as will every Master who resides on this side of the veil. Know that you house the power and grace to effect the greatest of change. So much more than I . . . so much more. Do you believe me? It is so.

My heart is filled with hope at what is about to happen on Earth. It is time for the old to fall away and the new to enter. It is time for those with negative intent to be pushed out, and those holding positive intent to rise up and lead. The entire cosmos supports you! Do you understand what I am saying? You do not act alone!!

So, please, young ones and your parents and elders, step up to the love plate, the peace plate, the God plate. Stop burying your head in the sand and hoping someone else will do the leading. There isn't anyone else more qualified than you to do this. You have incredible resources in us here, and in the power of Heaven! You cannot be stopped! It is your destiny to rework the present reality on Earth.

Abe [Lincoln] is here with me now and he is lending his support to the words that I am speaking. He is so excited at the idea of what you can do! You are all pure Light. You are greatness, each of you. Tap into that place within where you know yourselves as greatness. Tap into that place within where you know the inherent value of every individual.

I bow before you, citizens of the Earth. Each one of you is a sacred messenger of peace. Each one of you is a liberator of systems that no longer fit, of ways that are cruel, of abuse and tyranny. You are the holiest of beings and deserve to be honored for your work.

I am sending down my energy to assist you in your work. Abe sends down his, as well. This energy is backed by the Masters that surround us. We feel such reverence for you, you who have come to truly change the world. It is beautiful. You are all beautiful. Your mission is sacred.

What I see after this transformation is a glorious, shimmering planet with a vibration that is so high and pure that no negative thing can reside there. It won't take long, I assure you of that.

Get strong! Speak out! Trust in your greatness. Follow your heart. See your brothers and sisters as yourself. Carry them across the water and place them down gently on the other side, where they can know ease, joy, and fulfillment. Your hands are the hands of the Masters. They need you to do their work.

George and Abe and Jesus and Mary and Rama and Krishna and Buddha and all the others are here to offer encouragement and to praise a job well done. Because it IS done. It is done. In you, it is done.

ENDNOTES:

In my research I found that King was not focused solely on civil-rights issues in the United States. King was involved in global freedom and said that the U.S. should support "the shirtless and barefoot people" in the third world, rather than suppressing their attempts at revolution. In his speech on April 4, 1967, titled "Beyond Vietnam," he said, "There are people who have come to see the moral imperative of equality, but who cannot yet see the moral imperative of world brotherhood. I would like to see the fervor of the civil-rights movement imbued into the peace movement to instill it with greater strength. And I believe everyone has a duty to be in both the civil-rights and peace movements. But for those who presently choose but one, I would hope they will finally come to see the moral roots common to both."

On February 4, 1968, speaking about how he wanted to be remembered, King said, "I'd like somebody to mention that day that Martin Luther King Jr. tried to give his life serving others. I'd like for somebody to say that day that Martin Luther King Jr. tried to love somebody. I want you to say that day that I tried to be right on the war question. I want you to be able to say that day that I did try to feed the hungry. I want you to be able to say that day that I did try in my life to clothe those who were naked. I want you to say on that day that I did try in my life to visit those who were in prison. And I want you to say that I tried to love and serve humanity.

"Yes, if you want to say that I was a drum major, say that I was a drum major for justice. Say that I was a drum major for peace. I was a drum major for righteousness. And all of the other shallow things will not matter. I won't have any money to leave behind. I won't have the fine and luxurious things of life to leave behind. But I just want to leave a committed life behind."

Abraham Lincoln

May 22, 2015 — *Leap of Faith*

Yes, I am back. You know when I am around.

Lisa: Yes. It's a solemn feeling and I can see you.

Yes, I was rather solemn, serious. I still am, even over here. I am watching over this project, but I am also keeping an eye on humanity. It's not my job, per se, but I feel an inner urge to do so. Perhaps I haven't fully let go of the Earth and its destiny.

From up here, I see many changes happening. Most of them I see as good—even though there isn't really a sense of good and bad where I am; that's another carryover from my Earth life. So many people are demonstrating tolerance for things with which they, themselves, do not agree. That is a sure sign of evolution, both personally and collectively. It is inspiring to those of us watching the progress of your planet.

As MLK said last night, the young of your generation are indeed filled with more spirit than people of my time there were. It has been planned that way. Your destiny is to advance as a planet. Human consciousness is moving forward and the youth in your world will lead the way. They understand what MLK and I and many others did. They understand that they are part of a brotherhood, just as it is here. Everyone here works as a whole, loves as a whole, without class or race or gender. We here are without any kind of division or separation. We are as a whole here. Individual, in a sense, yes, but part of the whole. That is what is next for planet Earth.

In the not-too-distant future, there will be a sense of unity and care, care for one another and the planet itself. That is what is missing right now. Everyone believes that he is only working and living for himself and his immediate family, but that is not the case.

When Jesus walked the Earth, He attempted to open people's minds up to the concept of the brotherhood of man. He planted the seed. That seed grew into a plant throughout the centuries and now it is time to flower. The enlightened youth on your planet are the flowers and they are blooming full!

Adults, respect your young, for they carry within them more of what some call the Christ consciousness. They know what that term means. They know that it means peace, love, and unity, and that it includes all religions.

So respect these beautiful young souls. Pay attention to the things that they say to you. Listen to their ideas and their philosophies. The world as you know it is changing and they are the ones changing it. It is all according to plan. Things could not stay the same on Earth.

You would not have much of a planet left if you continued on in the same way as you are. It is time for a radical shift in perspective, consciousness. It is time for a remembering. It is time for a rebirth.

Adults, do not try to make your children like you; rather, try to be more like them! This world is going forward, not back. Let them be the example for you. Ask them to share their views with you. Learn from these wise souls. They will lead that world of yours into the next dimension of consciousness. Do not hold them back!

Youth, march forward in your truth! Blaze your own trail, despite what you are being taught by your teachers and society. Trust the information inside of yourself over anything taught to you by others. This is not to say that everything taught to you is wrong; it is not, but be discerning. When someone speaks to you, feel into it. See if it feels right to you, deep inside. Notice whether it makes your heart expand or shrink. Notice whether you feel uplifted by the information or not. Are the ideas being shared with you bringing you to a happier, more heart-centered place? Do they resonate with your inner knowing? Does the information unify or separate? You will easily know all these kinds of things. Check in with yourselves on everything you see and hear. Especially check inside when making all of your decisions.

In the deepest part of your hearts, you know the truth. This includes everyone on the planet, young and old. It is time to start living from that truth. It is time to stop denying what your heart knows. Let go of everything that was taught to you by society that does not resonate with the highest ideals of love and compassion, equality and justice.

The world is stepping forward and it needs all of you to participate in this great leap ahead. It is waiting for you. Are you ready?

Jayne Mansfield

May 25, 2015 — *Every Body Is Beautiful*

I feel very shy.

[*She was barely showing herself.*]

Funny, I wasn't this way in life at all! There was never an issue with showing myself then, but this feels different. It is so unusual. I didn't know this was even possible. Let me just take a moment to get more comfortable and step in closer.

[*I waited a while. I could feel her apprehension. She was still farther away when she began to talk.*]

I'll just start talking from here, if that is OK. As I feel more comfortable, I will move more into your line of vision. OK?

Lisa: Of course. I can hear you loudly and clearly regardless of where you stand.

As I peer down onto Earth, I realize I don't miss a thing. I mean, my family, yes, but many of them are here, of course. Other than my family, though, I don't miss it at all. There's so much drama, really! It's too much, to tell you the truth!

It's not even real, most of what we dramatize and fret over! It's so meaningless and unworthy of our time, it's almost ridiculous!

As I look down, it appears that people are like ants—building, building, building. And then one day, someone comes along and—*crush!*—steps on your creation. It's here today and gone tomorrow, so to speak.

So one thing I will say is this: don't get too attached to your possessions. They don't last—at all! Not only that, you may regret putting your energy and time into acquiring them, so what's the point? I am not suggesting that you don't have fun in life and enjoy material things. Of course, please do. Just don't give them more importance than they deserve. Don't cling to and hoard them. Be easy with them.

The thing I truly want to discuss is self-image. I speak mostly to the women who are reading this. I see a whole lot of people crying and dying over the look of their faces and bodies. No matter how beautiful or interesting or cute or sexy most women are, they see themselves as lacking in some way. It's sad, from this perspective.

Did you know that here, you are recognized only by your vibration? Just your vibration. And do you know how that vibration is created? By your heart. By your words and actions from all of your lifetimes. The color and vibratory rate of your energy determines your placement here. Not that anyone judges those higher or lower; there is no judgment or competition here. Everyone is happy with what she is and where she is, here. Not so, down there. All people are unhappy with what they are, there. Not *all* people of course, I am exaggerating, but so many people, mostly women, want to be different. They want to be better. They do not accept—never mind, love—who they are. They want to be smaller, or slimmer, or more voluptuous. They want to be firmer, fairer. I could go on and on.

It is hard to watch from up here. I can feel the angst as I attune to that field. It is a very far-reaching angst, across the continents, although some peoples in some areas and cultures are more accepting of themselves, which is nice to see. For the most part, however, people want to be something else. They want to look different.

Ladies, if you could see what matters here and how important it is to evolve your souls, you would not spend one more moment in angst over your physical selves. Do you know that there are planets where the beings all look the same? They design it that way so energy is not spent on comparison, judgment, and competition. They know that the soul's evolution is the important thing and so they eliminate that barrier. That is not likely to happen on Earth, but if I can help you to see how silly it is to focus on that aspect of yourself, I will feel justified in being chosen to speak today.

Women, you are beautiful exactly as you are right now. There is no need to starve yourselves, undergo surgery or change anything in any way. I speak from my own experience. I, like most women, believed I wasn't beautiful enough. The world considered me a glamour girl, a sex symbol, and yet I wasn't convinced. Do you see how this is? When you hold onto a belief, no evidence to the contrary will change that belief. If you hold within yourself the belief that you are unattractive or less attractive than you would like to be, you carry that around with you and no matter what anyone tells you, you will not see it. It's a sad state of affairs, isn't it? It traps you in a negative, lacking, unfortunate state.

You do this to yourselves. I realize that the media presents images of the current standard of beauty (that is set by those with an agenda), but it is you, ladies, who buy into it. You, and you, alone.

It is time to let all of that go! I wish I had learned to do that. Maybe I would've been happier had I done so, because no matter how attractive the world said I was, it was never enough. I didn't believe them most of the time. Even when I did believe them, I worried about losing my looks. I worried about aging. I wondered what I would have to offer the world when that happened. Those thoughts overwhelmed me.

Even when I did receive the praise, the world's praise for my beauty, it wasn't enough. I still felt insecure about my looks and felt competitive toward other women. I needed the attention. I couldn't enjoy the moment, so preoccupied was I with this. It was sad. My mental/emotional energy was focused in that direction most of the time, so I never truly lived. I regret it.

I want to help you. I would love to see you women truly participate in your lives. I would love to see you release your need to compete and let go of your feelings of envy, jealousy, and angst.

Just know that YOU can set the standard of beauty! It can be set to "NONE"! There is no standard of beauty in actual fact! Humans conceived that concept. Even those human standards vary from place to place on Earth.

I say, STOP! Start focusing on your inner selves. Evolve your souls.

Focus on what you CAN change about yourselves, and that is how you feel, how you see others, how you act. Change your priorities. Evolve yourselves to the point where you see not only yourselves as stunning, but all others too. Stop buying into another's impossible standard and killing yourselves to attain it. Send a clear message to other women and to the marketing companies that you are finished with any unnecessary abuse of self and that you refuse to be unfairly manipulated.

Start to embrace your inner essence. Notice your gifts and talents. Tap into the strength, wisdom, and love inside of yourselves and share that with others. Decide for yourselves that you won't accept anything less than total support and appreciation for who you are, whatever size and shape you happen to be, whatever look you happen to have. Honor each other as unique and beautiful.

To the men: You have been manipulated as well. You have given your power away to big business and other outside influences. At various times throughout history, heavier women were considered more attractive, as it is in some places today on Earth. These are changing trends only, and it is always someone outside of yourselves that decides what you are going to find attractive. Do you see?

You are energy beings, capable of seeing others with the eyes of the heart. Open THOSE eyes from now on. See inside the person you are with. Stop buying into society's changing ideals. Go deep inside of yourselves and find the person that you truly are—the loving, beautiful person who is there. Look inside for the part of you that accepts that beauty comes in all packages. Find the part of you that knows that beauty resides in the heart. To truly know happiness, you will have to accept yourselves and others as simply beautiful.

When each of you crosses over to this place, you will know that what

I'm saying is true. You will lament spending so much of your time feeling troubled over yourself, and the decisions that you made based on superficial things that vanished like puffs of smoke.

Love yourself. See beauty in yourself, in all others, and in all things. Let others know how beautiful they are. Pay no attention to the current, yet ever-changing beauty trends. Refuse to buy into "their" ideals. If you do this, it will end.

Begin to focus on the important aspects of yourself: the inner you, the eternal you, the true you. I wish I had . . .

ENDNOTES:

According to Hollywood historian and biographer James Robert Parish, Mansfield's hourglass figure (she claimed dimensions of 40–21–35), unique sashay, breathy baby talk, and cleavage-revealing costumes made a lasting impact on popular culture. A natural brunette, she had her hair bleached and became one of the "blonde bombshells." She was revered as Hollywood's gaudiest, boldest, B-grade actress from 1955 until the 1960s.

Throughout her career, Mansfield was compared to the reigning sex symbol, Marilyn Monroe. Jacqueline Susann wrote, "When one studio has a Marilyn Monroe, every other studio is hiring Jayne Mansfield and Mamie Van Doren." Mansfield was known as the "Cleavage Queen" and the "Queen of Sex and Bosom." But, as the 1960s approached, the female body ideal shifted to slim waiflike models like Twiggy and Audrey Hepburn. Mansfield died at the age of thirty-four in a car crash. She left five children.

Michael Jackson

May 26, 2015 — *Man in the Mirror*

What an awakening. Whew! This is nothing like what I expected. I don't know what I did expect, but this wasn't it.

I just feel so tired. I am here in what looks like an infirmary—a place like a hospital. I am working on restoring my energy field and healing the parts of me that were damaged by the substances I used. I'm resting. I'm getting lots and lots of rest.

I am not even ready to look back on my life. It's too soon for me. I am just happy to stay here. It was quite an interesting life and I feel like I would need more energy and strength to review it.

Here I am surrounded by the most beautiful beings. There is only peace and love and sweet energy here. It is . . . well, heavenly.

Why couldn't Earth have been like that? Why did it have to be so hard? I can hear some of you saying, "Hard? What was hard about YOUR life? You had money and success and adoration and literally anything you wanted." I can hear it, all right. And you would be right; I did have those things, but having things does not make a person happy inside. That was my problem: no inner joy.

I think my life started out that way. It's kinda sad, really. It wasn't any worse than a lot of others have experienced, but this isn't a competition. I'm just sharing that, as a youngster, the way I perceived the world—and that is a very good way to say it—was that it was a very sad place. I wasn't very happy inside as a child. That unhappiness just grew and grew over time.

The more I acquired, the more I felt it. Having so much made me feel guilty. Like how could a person with this much stuff be so sad? It was getting hard to look at myself in the mirror. There were times I got angry with myself over this. I berated myself over this question, because how could I? How could I be sad?

But here's the thing: stuff doesn't bring happiness. Neither tangible stuff nor intangible stuff. Nothing outside of yourself can make you happy. Nothing.

They say happiness is an inside job—and is it ever! I am still not feeling it, but at least I feel hopeful about attaining a peaceful state. I mean, how could I not be peaceful, being in a place like this?

It's so important that you don't judge anyone. It's been said that we shouldn't judge even the so-called good, because we don't know what's truly inside of a person, how real what you see on the outside is, and the extent of someone's path and challenges. It's not anyone's business to judge another. We shouldn't judge anything at all, not as good or bad. There's just no such thing at all, not here.

So, please, don't judge me or my life or my choices. I was fighting my own demons all along the way, as you are. It's just that you got to see me playing mine out. You don't have a public audience staring at you while you go through your struggles. But that's OK because it added to the growth factor for me. If I could go back, I would choose that same life, even as hard as it was.

There were also lots of good aspects to my life. It was a real drama, if you like dramas! It was never boring, that's for sure!

I think everyone should focus on him- or herself, and not on anyone else. There's enough to look at right there. Each of us has plenty of work to do just on ourselves, I'd say.

I don't blame any of you because I put myself in the spotlight and that was definitely the problem. I guess I wanted to walk my path while on display. That took some guts, I think. Hmmm . . . I never thought of myself as brave until just this second. Huh. I guess I was! That feels a little better.

Maybe that's the key—just noticing and appreciating the better parts of ourselves. You know how we mostly focus on the negative aspects of ourselves? We beat ourselves up for those things? Well, maybe the trick is to look more for the parts that are positive and then highlight those. I know that's easier said than done—is it ever! But this is sort of like an advice column here, from Heaven. So I would say that that's a very good piece of advice, one I should have followed. But it's never too late to "get" something and I just got something here: Notice what is right with yourself and highlight it. Spend more time on it, talking about it, focusing on it. Even bragging about it would be better, in my opinion, than ignoring and denying it, while we beat ourselves up over the negative crap that we believe we are. I mean, seriously.

OK, Lisa, I know that you have to go to an event, so we can end here and I will wait for your return. I'm not going anywhere! See, I'm funny too! That's another thing I didn't give myself credit for in life!

[*We resumed several hours later after I returned from my spiritual event.*]

How was your event?

Lisa: Great!

I should have done a little more spiritual seeking when I was there. It could've changed everything. I definitely identified with the body and the world too much, way too much. It would have been far better for me to have searched a little more for my spiritual identity. It's too late, though, for that lifetime, but there is always the next. And thank God too, because how can anyone be expected to get it all right the first time around? Or the second? Or even the hundredth?

If it's about having fun—and I don't yet know what the point of life is exactly—but suppose it is, then I can see why we do it again and again and again. So we can have more fun! As I see it from here, though, I didn't have much fun, this past life. So I'm not sure what the point was. Hmmmm . . . that is what I hope to learn here. What IS the point? I am sure I will be educated up here, but it would've been nice to have had some direction while down there.

When I watched what you were up to tonight, I kind of regretted not doing a little soul searching while down there. Maybe had I spent a little more time seeking the "inner" happiness that your friend Brian spoke of tonight, I would have lived a more peaceful, fulfilled life. Maybe that's my message, but I don't really feel qualified to give anyone messages or advice. I can only say what I wish I had done differently. If that has an impact on anyone reading, great; if it doesn't, that's OK too. All of you will find your own way as you need to, like me.

Who cares if we do it all right, according to our definition of "right," anyway? I think it's designed so that we get lots of opportunities to try things out. So maybe it's just OK, how things worked out for me. Maybe it's just fine. I think I will go with that for now. I mean, what else can I say, since I am just speculating here? It's like you and I have a conversation going here and I'm just processing things with you or something, while you type my words on your computer.

George [Harrison], was more together than I was. He had all the fame and fortune and everything that goes with it, but he didn't neglect his soul. He found a good balance, it seems. He had it together, you might say. When I see him up here, he seems like a holy man or something, in his white robes. I know you also see him that way, Lisa.

Lisa: Yes, that is exactly the way he shows up for me too. I always have to strain my eyes to see if it's him or Jesus coming toward me. Then he comes closer, and I see it's him. It's kind of cool.

Exactly. He does present just like that. I think he attained some kind of spiritual state down there. Or maybe he was that way before he took on the role of George Harrison, the Beatle, in that lifetime. Who knows?

I know that people down there are probably waiting for some profound—or at least, interesting—words from me, but I'm afraid I have nothing. I am just ordinary. Maybe that is the best thing I can offer: that I'm just ordinary. I'm nothing special at all, as the world would define "special," anyway, but we are all special here. That's the magic of this plane; everyone is the same, more or less, and yet we are each incredibly special. So it's more accurate to say that I *am* special, but not more than anyone else here.

There are different levels, it appears, but we are all loved and cherished the very same here. How nice is that? For someone like me who was so over-loved for the image that I projected there, it's nice to be ordinarily loved for who I actually am here. It's quite beautiful.

I think I will ask them here if I can hang out with George for a bit. We both lived similar lives in the same era. We can relate. I think I can learn something from him. I'm gonna ask if that would be OK, but I think they would be willing to have him visit me from time to time as I rest and regenerate.

Lisa, I've gotta hand it to you. You're seeking the right thing: soul growth. Seems you are on that track, and that feels so correct, as I see it from here.

I see you talk with Jesus quite a bit too. I might spend a bit of time with him, as well. I was drawn to him there for a time, but, as always, I got distracted from that whole thing. It was easy for me to do that— get caught up in the drama, the life of a superstar, and forget the rest. That superstar life can really mess with a person! It's really hard to see past it when you are living in it, day after day.

That biblical passage, "It's easier for a camel to go through the eye of a needle than for a rich man to enter the kingdom of God" should read, "It's easier for a camel to go through the eye of a needle than for a *superstar* to enter the kingdom of God." It is just so hard to let that identification go. It's almost impossible, at least for me.

I have a lot to clear away now. I have a lot of layers of ego identification to clear out. I also need to learn to let go of my faulty perceptions, and my regrets, and this self-punishment. It feels like a lot of work, but I'm ready. Perhaps it happens quicker than I'm thinking it does. See, that's the thing, I don't know much of how things work here so it's all speculation on my part. Sorry I can't be of more help. I am just so new here and really haven't been out of this area at all. The only reason I connected with George is because I heard the song you were playing [*"My Sweet Lord"*], and then I thought of him. It seems like he has some kind of job where he helps those over here to adjust in some way. That's what I'm feeling, anyway, so I'm excited to talk to him.

Maybe after I spend more time here, and get the healing that I need, or clearing, actually, I can talk to you some more and at that time, I might have some useful things to share. Could I come back possibly?

Lisa: Of course, I'd love that. I just want you to get what you need, whether that is rest or healing or clearing. I want that for you. Please know that what you have shared is very powerful. So thank you very much. Rest now, Michael.

Thank you, Lisa. You are kind. Thank you for connecting George and I, inadvertently. I think that will help me.

Good-bye for now. I hope to come again.

Lisa: You're welcome. Peace to you.

Jesus & George Harrison

May 29, 2015 — *One*

[*I noticed them coming in together at other earlier times and sometimes I didn't know which one was which until they got closer and one stepped back while the other one came forward. It seemed odd to me, but I didn't question it.*]

Jesus: Yes, Lisa, we are coming in together tonight. That song you are listening to is so appropriate for this visit.

Your heart feels full right now—full of love. That is my presence and vibration that connects you to this state. Lisa, I want you to know that you, and all of you reading, can attain that state anytime that you wish.

Going to an altar, being in nature, holding someone you love, all of these things can help connect you to the love vibration. But, dear

Lisa, it is always inside of you. In fact, it is what you are made of. You are constructed out of love cells. Pure love. All of you are. All of your being is love, pure love. Anything else is just a distortion that appears real. Love alone is your essence.

Do you know how simple it is to tap into that truth?

Lisa: No. It feels pretty hard sometimes. Impossible, even, at times.

Yes, amid your chaotic lives, it does take some effort. The effort is in moving that which is distortion out of the way. And the distortion is that you are separate from Source, and from each other.

Every living thing is just an aspect of you; that is it. Whether someone offends you, or pleases you, it's all the same. It's you. Do not point your finger at your so-called enemies and blame them for their attack on you. Rather, realize what honestly took place: a part of yourself wanted to be loved. It's simple.

You are right now feeling confused and hurt over someone's treatment of you. You cannot understand how they could have been so manipulative, false, and passive-aggressive toward you. Lisa, do you know that those others are only aspects of yourself that you have created for the sole purpose of loving them into wholeness? At this time, you see those people—and if you believe what I am saying, those aspects of yourself—as separate from the whole of you, yet they are not.

This experience is a blessing from yourself, for yourself. You brought them into being simply so that you could look at them, acknowledge them as a part of yourself, and accept those parts of yourself with love and allow them to stay. They are needed to make up the whole. When they are loved and cherished, as with the "good" aspects of yourself, they will cease to be, as they will simply blend together with all aspects of your being, into love. You came from love; you end up in love. In love, you live. Inside of that love is everything, every single thing possible. So how could any of it be less than love, even if it appears to be, when it belongs to love, when it IS love?

All expressions of yourself, whether you determine them to be good or bad, are simply love. The way those expressions manifest is through the appearance of others. That is how it is designed.

So when you see someone doing something that isn't to your liking, realize as quickly as you can that they are only a divine expression of your very own self, wanting to be seen. Embrace and love all aspects that you see revealed in these others.

So let us go back to these two people in your life by whom you recently felt hurt. First, look at them. See for yourself. Those are parts of yourself that just want to be seen. Like a badly behaved child, he or she is only trying to be seen—and loved. So see them, and then love them. Call them to come closer to you, rather than push them away. Call to them. Look deeply into their eyes. Know that they stand before you wanting to be acknowledged, loved, and accepted. When you do that, you will feel a transformation happen, just like you would if you did this with an unruly child.

What do you think would happen to a child who was kicking and screaming, if you just smiled and spoke sweetly to him? If you cooed at him? If you invited him into your arms and hugged him and stroked his hair, while telling him how much you love him? If you held him in love without any resistance, irritation, anger, or frustration, just peaceful love, what do you suppose would happen? He would settle down and melt into your arms and into your love.

So it is with these unruly people, or aspects of yourself, that you see around you. Those who appear to hurt you, steal from you, manipulate you, or lie to you will melt into the love that you are the moment you smile at them, speak sweetly to them, call them closer, invite them into your arms, and tell them how much you love them. They will melt into oneness with you.

Would you like to try that now to see what happens?

Lisa: OK. [I proceeded to go into a big healing process that took some considerable time.]

How was that?

Lisa: It was very deep and emotional. I started out imagining those two people with whom I was angry. I saw them in front of me. I softened my heart, just like you asked, and found myself loving them. I called them to me, held them, and stroked their hair as I said things to them like, "I love you so much. You are beautiful." All of my negative feelings toward them disappeared and I felt that we blended together in love.

From there, I was guided backward in time to when I was a child, and through times in my life when I was mean, hurtful, bullying, manipulative, and downright nasty in my thoughts and actions toward others. I was taken through the main scenes, going right into each one, witnessing myself doing or saying these hurtful things.

In each case, I decided to look upon that Lisa—whether child Lisa, teenager Lisa, or adult Lisa—with compassion, seeing that part of myself as simply a hurt, sad, or attention-seeking aspect of myself that needed love. I did not focus on the "bad" they were saying or doing; rather, I simply looked at them with deep love and beckoned them to come to me. I invited them to sit on my lap, while I stroked their hair, and soothed them with my love and kindness, telling them how precious they are, how beautiful and perfect they are. I told them how special they are, and that I could not live without them. They calmed down in my arms and let me love them. It felt so nurturing and soothing to the soul.

It was very powerful, Jesus, because up until now, I had always hated myself for the things that I had done in my life that caused pain to others—and there were many because I was a very angry, hurt person. I finally really, truly forgave myself, without having to say, "I forgive you." I just loved myself into forgiveness.

Then the coolest thing happened! Each of the people who were in the scenes as my abused, suddenly became me! Just as you said: everybody is us! They became me, and smiled at me, and casually walked away, as if they had just finished a rehearsal in which they were playing a role or doing a job, and were done for the day. They each gave me a look as if to say, "See how it all works!"

It was so intensely healing, Jesus! Thank you! I can see now that they ARE all me: the abuser and the abused. There is no separation, no "other," there is just me. I will try very hard to remember this going forward. I will try to see all of the people in my life simply as parts of myself that are acting out scenes to get my attention, to get my love and acceptance.

Thank you so very much for that experience!

You are welcome. That is one of the things that people suffer with the most: the sense of separation from each other and from God. Thank YOU for doing the exercise! When any one of you makes a shift toward love, everyone benefits.

Lisa: I need to ask why George is here since he hasn't said anything.

George: I have asked if I could shadow Jesus. I want to learn directly from Him. Think of it as an apprenticeship program, a "job shadowing." I want so much to grow in my capacity to love and serve, and who better to learn from than this Master? This Master, by the way, is all of the Masters rolled into one. I could as easily have called Him "Buddha" or "Krishna," or by any one of the other Masters' names. They're one and the same. It's just that you, Lisa, like to separate them out. Ha-ha! That's funny, isn't it? Separating even the Masters! They are all one being. WE are all one being. Everyone. Do you see?

So, yeah, I have requested that I be allowed to come along with Jesus and learn the ropes, you could say, while he talks to you down there, and maybe also in His exchanges with others. I love this! I think I may come back as a preacher in my next life! Hmmm . . . but by the time I get back there, things are gonna look very different than they are now. Humans are going to be further along in their remembrance of the truth of whom they are, so there won't be as many preacher positions available, ha-ha! Everyone is moving toward being his or her own preacher—as it should be.

I guess I'm not sure what will be next for me but I am learning now, here, and it fills me with happiness and fulfillment.

I'm so glad you let me listen in. By the way, I love the music you are playing right now. It's beautiful. [*Deva Premal's "Gayatri Mantra"*]

Thank you again for doing this. I think there are some powerful messages here in this book and I am grateful to have been part of it. Maybe I will see you again.

Jesus: Blessings on you, Lisa, for having the courage to look at those things that had been hidden from view. You've done a great job. Keep it up! If you need a hand with it in the future, you know I'm here to help. I am here to help anyone who calls on me. It is my greatest joy to be in loving service to all.

In Light and Love.

John Lennon

May 30, 2015 — The Revolution Starts with the Evolution Within

We could almost start a band over here—George, Davy, and some of the others! I'm joking, but it could almost be done. Anything's possible here, you know.

OK. I was invited to be part of this because they think I have something to say. I have lots to say, but I'm not sure what is most important. Let's see . . .

I did try in my lifetime to bring deeper messages to the world. I guess that is still my agenda. So that is what I will speak to first: the brotherhood of man. If you could see how things work around here—EVERYONE helps one another. EVERYTHING is based in love. It's an "all for one and one for all" kind of mind-set—or should I say heart-set—here. It's beautiful, people!

Lisa, I can see that you're tired now, as it is late, so I'm happy to come back in the morning and continue. I have so much to say, I now realize.

For now, let me say good night, and I look forward to connecting again in the morning.

Lisa: Good night and thanks, John.

June 6, 2015

You are praying before each session that you bring in clear, relevant, truthful, accurate information. Because your purpose is to help raise consciousness on Earth, we, the chosen ones, are speaking on important topics, not just nonsense. You worry that no one will want to read what we have to say, but the vibration of this work will be such that people will find it. They will benefit from it. You can stop worrying about this.

I loved my girl. We were destined to meet. We found each other in that lifetime, just as we'd planned. Sometimes when two people come together, it is just meant to be. I mean, *meant!* That no matter where or how your individual lives are progressing, there is a destiny to be played out and you will collide. That is what happened for us. It was "written."

We often felt like we were in a world of our own; sometimes we wished we were. I had enormous pressure on me to be "out there," to partake in "the life." I would have enjoyed being on a deserted island with her. I would have enjoyed running away with her. She feels me around her. She knows I am not far away. She still feels my energy loving and surrounding her. Thank God! I love her and my sons.

They are my loves.

My sons think of me often and I want them to know that I am there, right with them. I am so proud of them. I'm so pleased with the men they have become.

I want to say that I forgive the man who cut short my life. It's total forgiveness that I offer to him. It was all meant to be this way. He has my full and free forgiveness. If I can forgive him, I ask everyone else to do the same.

When Jesus spoke to you the other day, Lisa, and told you that everyone is just a reflection and projection of ourselves, he was dead on. It was as it should be for me to leave the planet at that time. What a gift this man is offering to the world. He is giving you all the opportunity to do something that is so difficult for you to do, but absolutely necessary. He's giving you the chance to dig deep into your hearts and find that part of yourselves that loves unconditionally, that even loves those who reflect the "bad" parts of yourselves. We are made up of all of it: the good AND the bad. We contain the entire universe. That does not mean only the lovely parts; it's the universe in its entirety.

I often displayed the darker aspects of myself. I have had to learn here to accept and love those aspects too. It's all me. I ask you to forgive and love the man who fulfilled my destiny. He is pure love, as we all are.

Cultivate peace in your hearts. Love everyone, regardless of whether they love you in return. It is the act of loving that is important.

I had such a struggle in my lifetime with the shadow and light sides of myself. They were warring with each other regularly. It's like the story where a man, describing his own inner struggle says, "Inside of me, there are two dogs. One of the dogs is mean and evil. The other dog is good. The mean dog fights the good dog all of the time." When asked which dog wins, he reflected for a moment and replied, "The one I feed the most."

Well, sometimes I fed the mean one and sometimes, the good. I operated out of my light side AND my shadow. Both are real. Both are acceptable. Both are me. And you.

Start to love yourselves, deeply, as I have. It is my work over here just to learn love, starting with myself. It will move from me—or you—to the whole world. Then, what a world we shall have!

I am so at peace here. I am learning and growing and loving. I watch over my family—my human family and my Earth family. I will help in whatever way I can because this, too, is my destiny.

Peace to all of you.

[*He showed me a heart.*]

Davy Jones

June 3, 2015 — *Shift Your Focus; Change Your Life*

[*I can feel Davy wanting to pop in for a quick second.*]

Lisa: Hi, Davy! You back?

Why, yes, I can't get enough of this!

[*I cannot stop smiling; his energy is just delightful—so cheery and happy. I love it!*]

It's not that I'm bored over here or anything. There's no such thing as boredom here. It's just so interesting, talking like this and being able to connect from here to there. You know what I'm saying? Just so cool!

I know I said that it's so incredible here, and it is! But don't underestimate what your place is. It's real great too! It's just what you make it. It's what you choose to make of it. You see, you can get all bogged down in the stress and challenges there, the real human-suffering kind of stuff. And fair enough, it's there, all right. I KNOW! But as difficult as it might be to shift your focus, DO! As often as you can.

Your time just flies by down there, even though it might not feel like it at times—until you're old, that is. But it does! So why waste any of it sinking deep in despair or stressing about things you can't change. It's not worth it AT ALL!

Try, instead, to look around it. Literally, look around whatever issues you are facing. Look into the future, reminding yourself that in fifty years or seventy-five years, it's not gonna matter anymore, so why worry about it? Try your best to just observe things without getting too attached to the illusion that your life dramas are. They are dramas and illusions, as someone else said here. That's the truth. So why get all worked up over things? Why make yourselves sick, or lose friends over it, or keep yourselves in a state of sadness, anger, or stress? For what? For this illusion? For something that is NOT going to matter one whit a few years later? Just live! Try to breeze through life a little easier, with a little more softness and a lot more joy!

That's what I'm trying to bring to this little party here—my two cents. I hope it helps just one person let go of his or her heaviness and instead enjoy more of his or her lighter side. One person would be enough for this cat.

OK, I think someone else might want to come in to see you, Lisa, so I will sign off here. I thank you again for being open to me and receiving me so well, with all that bubbly joy you feel from me. I feel it from you, too. We vibe each other! THAT'S what I'm talking about: grab the joy! What a way to go through life!

See ya, Lis.

Lisa: Thank you, Davy. You know, don't you, that that nickname is very special to me. My beloved sister, Kim, called me "Lis." Very few others have called me that. It warms my heart and brings a huge smile to my face because you made me think of her. You knew I'd like it, didn't you?

Yep, I did. Just wanted to make that beautiful smile of yours even brighter!

Lisa: Thanks!

You're welcome. See ya later!

[I was playing "My Sweet Lord" and I could see him dancing away from me. What a great dancer! He's so fun!]

Edgar Cayce

June 3, 2015 — *Connection Is Key*

[*Davy danced away from me, leaving me feeling wonderfully uplifted. But not for long. Soon, I felt a presence around me that felt quite the opposite. This spirit was heavy and somewhat sad and serious. What a contrast! I soon realized it was Edgar Cayce. I didn't know what kind of man he had been in real life, so I wondered why the heaviness and sadness.*]

Yes, it is me. And yes, I am feeling sad. It just seems that people are getting further and further from the truth. I know that is not what some of your other guests observe, but I do. I look around down there and I am dismayed to see less interaction as families and communities than when I was alive. That troubles me. In this age of the Internet, yes, you can have lots of friends in lots of faraway places, but these relationships seem shallower—going wide, not deep.

That is the opposite of what is needed in your world.

Deep connectivity is needed where you are, in order to move this race forward. It's not a time to hide behind your individual computers and isolate; it's a time to gather together to create solutions to the issues facing you as a people. And to create harmony, understanding, and a united front.

You have the tremendous power of your young people; that is true. I can see that they are doing more than their share by simply holding ideas of truth inside of themselves. That is the positive and the negative, right there, you see. Because while they house all of this truth, most of them are keeping those truths inside of themselves. They are getting caught up in the new trend of disconnection.

Lisa, I can hear your thoughts. You disagree with me. You think that the young people are so close to one another and comfortable expressing love to one another, and you take that as a sign that they are embracing the concept of togetherness. But while they DO have oneness-attuned minds and hearts, they are actually living in a more isolated way than in any other time. I speak here mostly of the first-world countries. In the others, they continue to value clan and community.

It's just a trend that I have observed, and however it started, and for whatever reason, I just feel sad seeing it. I would love to see the young people give more attention and devotion to each other and less to their electronic devices, which seem to be replacing actual people, actual relationships.

I don't want to focus entirely on this aspect of people because, indeed, there are a lot of positive things happening. I see this also. I guess I just want to point this out so that it might receive some attention. Perhaps it will get people thinking a little, is all.

The people with whom you sit down to eat are precious. You can learn from them, enjoy them, and love them. They enrich your lives. I would like to see people put down their phones and look at the people with whom they are walking, dining, communicating.

Maybe try to notice the disassociation that is being played out all over the place. Try association. Choose connection. It will significantly improve your lives. You see, in your world, you are all feeling hungry, empty. Your souls are all seeking deep connection, Divine connection. It's what you all ache for, long for, wish for. Deep, deep inside of yourselves, this is your genuine want and need. Yet, you do the very things that prevent this from occurring. You put up one barrier or another between yourselves and others, between your wish and your reality.

It's not a difficult thing to change. It's really very easy, actually. Simply look at those around you. Talk to them, person to person. Deeply communicate with them, finding out how they are and helping them with the things that trouble them. Enjoy earthly pleasures with them. Smile genuinely at each other. Form real bonds. Spend real time together, with no distractions to pull you away from one another. Make a point of doing these things, and watch what happens.

I feel heavy about this because I thought the world was moving in such a positive direction around the time that I lived. Positive, in the sense that there seemed to be a draw toward the spiritual. That is happening now, as well, I can see. I notice the openness with which people are exploring various spiritual paths. It's just that spirituality isn't found on the top of a mountain all alone. Not to say being on top of a mountain can't bring you to a high spiritual place, because it can, but you are there on Earth to do more than attain this state. You are there to embody it, to live it with others. You are there to share it with others. Does that make sense?

I will let that topic go now because I know that you, Lisa, want to let that emotion of mine go. You can feel it in me, I know. Hmmm. Just before I came in, Davy talked about NOT going into the heaviness and staying in the joy, which is your preferred state, I know! So I will "snap out of it" now!

I AM impressed by how open people are nowadays—open-minded, open-hearted. I'm impressed by how tolerant everyone has become. THAT I can celebrate! How wonderful! It's just a matter of time before the whole world lives in peace and unity. It's coming, people! It will happen faster if you connect deeper with one another now! OK, there I go again.

I think I will go back now and perhaps come again another day, if it seems appropriate. Either way, it was a blessing to come through and share my views with all of you. Thank you for allowing me to do so.

Good-bye, all.

Mark Twain

June 4, 2015 — The Party Starts When Everybody Goes Home

Well, I never imagined myself doing this! This is incredibly interesting! I feel like a schoolboy, just hearing about something brand-new, and being excited about the discovery! It's hard to believe that you are connecting in with me and my thoughts, and transcribing them. This is really something wonderful.

I will try to speak—I mean, think—slowly so that you can keep up.

Lisa: Thank you, Mark; that is very sweet and thoughtful of you to consider me. I will be OK though, so just be yourself; be natural. But, thank you.

How different things are down there. I hardly recognize the place! I am not sure if I was lucky or not, living when I did.

Things were unquestionably more difficult in my time, yet in many ways, it seemed easier. As I look at your world now and compare it to when I was there, things seem more convoluted, complex, and stressful presently—even with all your modern conveniences, gadgets, and technology. I'm not sure what to make of it all. I've been quite peaceful over here so I haven't bothered to even take a peek down there since I arrived. I may need a bit of time to survey, if you will.

Lisa: Take your time.

A lot of what I see, as I peer down, is just activity. I suppose that is the thing that strikes me the most. Was it always that busy on Earth? Maybe it always has been, but when you are in it, you don't notice. Perhaps it's only once you step away that you can see the movement that seems so frantic. Everyone is on the move. There is hardly any rest.

I'd say that is the biggest difference between our two worlds: the intensity with which you people move and live! Here, it is nice and slow and deliberate and restful. Even the "doing" is restful and pleasant. Everyone is at peace here. We are busy doing things, but the feeling of peace and tranquility prevails. So much happens but it is strangely calm, like that music you are playing now. That music is so rich and full and complex in the most gentle way. [*Deva Premal's "Gayatri Mantra"*]

That is how everything is here: beautiful, especially beautiful. It's the kind of beautiful that would make you cry if you could see it. It's a wonder any of us ever want to leave here! Truly. I am amazed that we long for the Earth experience. I am not sure I am going back. I believe we have the choice, and I'm considering staying on.

I was a very sensitive fellow while in my last incarnation, and I continue to feel everything in my environment deeply. I sensed things very acutely on Earth and that made it a struggle to maintain myself in the Earth atmosphere. The conditions here resonate strongly with me. I'm a match for this energy; it suits me better, so I may elect to stay.

Now, I'm not so sure I will stay right here in this exact location. I have an inner urge to explore what is here in this afterworld, to go traveling, I suppose one could say. That is what is so beautiful: anything—and I do mean, anything—you want, you can have here. Nothing is denied you. And I feel like exploring around a little. I'm getting ready to do that, and I'm eager to be on my way.

You see, there is no boredom here. Action, adventure, and learning are all options here. However, unlike on Earth, it is done in a graceful, refined way. That's a good word for it: "graceful." Like the movement of a ballerina, soft and graceful.

To those of you who fear death, oh, please believe me when I say it is bliss, incredible bliss. You won't believe the exquisite bliss that is this place. There are no human words that can convey accurately what this is like. The divine beauty of this sacred dwelling place simply cannot be described. I apologize for my lack of words here. It must be experienced; that is all I can tell you.

I am not sure what is expected of me, regarding my contribution to this work. It seems that the only thing I can share, honestly, is my deep joy and contentment with my state of being and living at the present time.

Perhaps I am speaking directly to those that do fear the transition. They may be facing death at this very moment. If that is so, I say, let your mind be at peace, let your body go, let your spirit fly to this paradise. It is more exquisite than anything you could ever imagine. It is glorious. It truly IS Heaven. And once you experience this ecstasy for yourself, you may never want to leave. So just let go.

For those of you not facing immediate death, live your life there to the fullest. Let your life overflow with goodness and joy, excitement, passion, and adventure, and do not hold within yourselves any fear of this place, for it is sublime.

With that, I bid you adieu.

[*A little bit later. he continued . . .*]

Lisa, I pray that what I have shared here is valuable. I would never want to take up space in your book when others could have more wisdom to impart. If you feel it is not important enough, please leave it out. I am not attached either way; I just want what is best for everyone.

Lisa: Mark, what you have said here is immensely valuable. So many people, most I would guess, have a fear of death. It's the great unknown. And your honest, gentle sharing will, undoubtedly, ease minds and bring hope to those who need it. I am very grateful for your insights and information, very grateful.

On a personal note, I appreciate being in your energy field while channeling you; you have such tranquil energy, just lovely, really. Thank you for letting me experience that aspect of you. I dare say, I need it, as I am definitely living one of those frantic lives of which you spoke! Thank you. Enjoy that Heaven of yours!

Good-bye.

Good night, Lisa, and thank YOU.

ENDNOTES:

Mark Twain was psychic, predicting his brother's and his own death. He was part of the first psychical research groups. He liked modern conveniences, gadgets, and technology. He was a world traveler for most of his life.

Abraham Lincoln

June 6, 2015 — *Out of Many, One*

[*I could feel Lincoln coming back in. I felt teary.*]

What does it say on the penny?

[*I had to go and look because while I knew it said "In God We Trust," I felt that he was referring to something else.*]

Lisa: It says, "In God We Trust." On the other side, it says, "E PLURIBUS UNUM," which translates to "Out of many, one."

Precisely. Out of many, one. That is the most important thing to remember here: "Out of many, one."

Those words can have many meanings, but the one I am most interested in here is that, at the core of everything, we are just one being. We are one heart, one mind, one supreme intelligence, one direction, one path. One. One. One. We are not separate from one another in any way. We share the same vital energy. We originate from the same Source. We end up back with that same Source. It just appears, for a time, that we are separate. Do not be fooled, you ARE your brother. You ARE your sister. You ARE the man next door, and your child. There is no difference between you and those you call "others." If you could try today to understand this truth, and live it, you would be better off for it, as would your world. Out of many, one. That is beautiful. Live this.

I want to clarify, Lisa, what this project is about. It is not to be about entertaining people, as you thought it would be. There is plenty of entertainment in your world already; there is no need for more. No, it is intended to speak to the soul, reminding people of important things that they may have forgotten. We chose famous people to deliver these essential messages—"reminders," you might say—because we knew that the messages would reach a wider audience that way. The messages are all that is important, ultimately.

We, here, on this side, do not value earthly fame. It is meaningless, illusory. It was not important even on Earth, although some of us got lost in it for a time. But that fame had no true value even there on Earth. It certainly is not valued here. Everyone is equal once they cross planes, as is appropriate and correct. That is our true state: equality.

Lisa: Abe, I am feeling tired as it is almost two o'clock in the morning. Would you mind if we continue this later in the morning?

I understand completely. Whenever you would like to continue, just call on me. I will be ready and available.

Lisa: Thank you so much for your understanding. Good night.

Good night.

June 11, 2015

It is me; I am back. I didn't come back sooner because you were not in the right frame of mind to work on this. You seemed bogged down with your earthly concerns.

Lisa: Yes, I knew that was what you were thinking, and how true. Thank you for noticing and respecting my life here.

You're welcome, Lisa.

We are just about through here, on this project, but not quite. There are a few others who we feel might be good additions. They have important things to say. It's not much longer before we conclude.

I will say good night for now and wait until those others who may wish to come in, do, and then I will conclude. Good night, Lisa.

Lisa: Good night, Abe.

John Wayne

June 13, 2015 — *I Used to Be a Hawk; Now I'm a Dove*

Howdy, Lisa! Do you like that? Ha-ha, just kidding with you!

[I felt sad even though he was kidding with me.]

I feel melancholy. There are so many things I would do differently if I could live my life again. I am not sure I'll get that chance. I haven't been told anything about "what's next" here. I am just resting and reviewing my last lifetime as "John Wayne."

That was a persona, one I grew into, at that. I didn't start out being John Wayne. I had a lesser-known side to me, before I "became" that role. I was sensitive to others, gentler, more caring, not so much the "he-man." It was like I grew into the role and became it. I forgot my true identity during those famous acting years. That is what I am melancholy about.

You see, I didn't live what you like to call "my truth." I just parked my former self somewhere and adopted a whole new persona. After a while, I didn't even remember my former self. I guess I will never know what would have become of me had I not taken the path that I did, although, here, they are very good about showing us potential life paths. I have chosen not to look. It might be too sad for me.

You see, what I valued down there, strength and force, mean nothing now. It was a false strength, based on fear, really, that was driving me. Of course, I didn't realize any of that while living it. It's only here that that has become clear.

The human definition of strength is wrong; what we value as strong isn't worth a damn! Might, power, force—they're all based in fear. It's fear of being controlled or taken over. It's fear of losing something. Fighting for position, importance, land, relationships, money, anything at all, is pointless. What a damn waste of time, I see now!

I could have cultivated real strength during my time there. "What is real strength?" you may ask. It is the strength to be oneself, the strength to walk in integrity with oneself. It is the ability to be generous with others, without fear that you will be left wanting. I was very possessive with my things, with all of my things. I didn't want to share with too many people. I mean that on a personal level and also on a grander scale. I was territorial. I wanted to keep things separate.

I am learning here that there are no borders, boundaries, or differences separating us. That thinking originates in the human fear-based mind. Well, I won't speak for all humans! There are many great human minds, highly conscious people who understand what I am learning here. To them, my hat's off!

I guess I was not at that level of awareness when I was down there.

They tell me here that it's all OK, that we are all on our own personal journey of discovery and recall. But I just feel regretful that I didn't learn some of this while I was down there. As I review my life from this realm, I feel like many of the things that I argued for, fought for, supported, and spoke out against were in error, at least, as I see it from here. And believe me, I don't have the answer to everything yet, but I know I am a lot closer to the truth than I was down there, while I was operating out of my fear-based mentality.

That is why, Lisa, I joined you last night at that spiritual event you were participating in. I know you were surprised to see me because you thought the project might be done, but no, it isn't!

Even then, when you got home from the event and it was so late, I was pushing my way in. I knew you were tired. You even, at one point, told me to wait until today when you were rested, but I didn't leave you alone. I apologize. I guess I am still pushing my way here and there! I used to push my attitudes on people. I used my life and influence to persuade others to come to my way of thinking. In retrospect, I see that it wasn't the highest path to take.

I am adopting a much more elevated consciousness here. Well, I'm on my way toward understanding and adopting one, I should say. Long way to go! LONG way to go! But hell, it looks like we have all the time in the world once we get here, so . . .

I don't want you to think I joined you today simply to lament my choices while I was alive. That isn't quite it. While it is important that I share my feelings with you, I do want to help people in a real way. I want them to benefit from my newly acquired wisdom. Ha! All kidding aside, Lisa, I do think I have some valuable insights to share. If not, readers can skip on over my chapter and read a better one! I won't be offended, people!

Yes, you are smelling tobacco, Lisa. [*The smell was suddenly so strong.*]

I will speak directly to the reader now: First off, take care of your bodies, everyone! You only have one and it's gotta last a very long time! There are a lot of things that you are doing and you know full well that they hurt your body, so stop. Just stop! Use whatever methods you need to, to help with this, but just stop. Get hypnotized. Use therapy. Use twelve-step programs or alternative healing methods. Use prayer or discipline or whatever works. There are new things coming out daily; try them! That takes care of the body.

Second, cleanse your mind and heart of all bigotry, racism, hatred, mean-spiritedness, and judgment. Purify yourselves. Again, find ways to do this. Even the spiritual exercises I observed at last night's gathering were wonderful for such things.

Then, cultivate within yourselves higher qualities, ones that people admire, such as tolerance, kindness, patience, generosity, love, and grace. And *real* strength. Not the human fear-based strength and power—that's a load of crap; I'm talking about true power. That is the power to be true to yourself and your path, to stand in your integrity. The power to forgive what you consider to be a wrong. The power to be vulnerable and share your fears with others. The power to look at yourselves deeply and honestly and make amends, changes, and adjustments when you have erred in your thinking or actions. And the power that allows you to honor all others without fear of losing anything.

Does this sound silly to you, any of you? Because, listen, when you're where I am, it's the only thing you'll be working on, the only thing you'll care about! Mark my words! You're gonna get to it, one way or the other; I'm just giving you a heads-up, is all. I mean, I can only imagine how drastically your lives would improve if you did some of this stuff while you were still down there. I just wish someone had gotten through to me while I lived. But, hey, like I said, we all get to it one way or the other—and I'm gettin' to it now!

To my children and grandchildren, I wish I had left a legacy of love behind, rather than just a pile of movies. I feel proud of my success in the movie industry; don't get me wrong. It's just that I could have been so much more. I was a force—yeah, there's that word again—but by earthly standards I WAS a force, an influence, and had I been stronger, braver, and more spiritually aware, I suppose, I could have done so much more for the world than I did. Then I'd have left so much more behind.

Anyway, I will conclude by saying, all is not as it seems. What you, there, value as true and right, is not necessarily so, here. Open yourselves to learning more of the truth while you are there, and take that truth and use it to advance yourselves right away, while you are still in human form. Don't wait, people!

I am done here. Thank you for having me, Lisa.

Lisa: You are welcome, John. Thanks for sharing and thanks for popping in last night. Feel free to join in on whatever future events interest you. Bye.

See ya later, Lis.

Shirley Temple Black

June 13, 2015 — *Life Is Like a Lollipop; Lick It till It's All Gone*

[*Feeling sadness*]

Yes, Lisa, it's Shirley Temple. I know how much you love my movies, even as an adult. You are thinking of watching one tonight, now, aren't you?

I do feel sad tonight as I come to you. I miss my children very much. I can hardly look away from their beautiful faces. I am reunited with my husband and many other loved ones, which is so wonderful, really so wonderful, and yet the longing to be near my children remains. They say here that it will ease up, and I do hope they are right.

I would like to give them a direct message: All of you, my children, grandchildren, and great grandchildren, were the best part of my life. The love and joy that you brought into my life is immeasurable.

I carry that love and joy with me still. I am never without it. I never will be. I will be with you, all of you, always. I remain close to each one of you; remember that, my darlings.

It is true, Lisa, that we, on this side, can be with our loved ones, and what a precious gift that is, but not having the physical connection is an adjustment, nevertheless. I am told that in time, it will get easier, and I will feel freer to move about, but for now, I like to stay close. Thank you for sending my message out to them.

As I reflect on my life, I'd say my only sadness was not being able to enjoy a normal childhood. It was far from normal, as you can imagine. That isn't to say that I didn't have some good, fun moments as a child, I just didn't get to have the full experience of being a child. I had to grow up and operate in the adult world as a wee girl, but I suppose it's a trade-off isn't it? I lost my childhood, which I regret, but I gained recognition and fame that helped me realize many of my personal dreams and ambitions. So I was OK with it, ultimately.

But that is why I went to great lengths to ensure that each of my own children had as normal a childhood as possible, given the circumstances. I did my best to give them all that I missed. I hope I succeeded, because it was my deep desire to do so.

I believe, despite the things lacking in the early part of my life, that my life was wonderful. It truly was, Lisa. I had so many advantages and opportunities, more than most, and I strove to benefit from those advantages and make the most of those opportunities. I wanted to make my time count, you might say. I feel that I succeeded for the most part. Oh, did I do everything I set out to do? Absolutely not. But I feel content with what I did do in my life, such that I can speak to you now without regret. That is so important, I feel. It's so important to be able to live one's life in such a way that you leave without many regrets, if any at all.

How one does that is very personal. There is no better or worse way to live life. It's personal. For some, it may be a career path that they are committed to. For others, it is following an artistic passion. For others, it is finding and enjoying great personal love relationships. For others still, it is something altruistic. Perhaps it is a little of each. Whatever your ideal life consists of, it is simply important to stay on course with it so that at the end, you'll feel that your life has been well lived.

I think it is important not to rely on anyone to make that happen. Try not to blame anyone for what you perceive as a disadvantage. No one has the power to stop your life from unfolding in the way you dream it. They may put temporary roadblocks up in front of you, causing you to stumble a little, but ultimately, you are responsible for regaining control of your life and pressing on. I would say that is the most important thing that I can share today. That it is your life and that you, and only you, make it great, fulfilling, meaningful, and rich . . . or not. No matter what has happened in your life—or what is happening currently—remember who is in charge. Remember whose life it is and do your best to live it on your terms, according to your dreams and intentions.

I believe I am finished for now. If I have more to say, I may ask to come back, if that is OK.

Lisa: Yes, of course.

Thank you for having me here, and, most especially, for affording me the opportunity to connect with my loved ones there. They are so dear to me, Lisa. My heart just overflows with love for them. I am sending waves of this love down to them at this very instant. Thank you ever so much for bringing this message to these dear ones of mine. I am eternally grateful.

Lisa: It is my honor to do so, Shirley. Thank you for trusting me with it. Blessings to you and yours.

Jane Russell

June 15, 2015 — *Let Your Guard Down*

Yes, you are right; it's Jane. Another Jane. I know you don't really want to channel me, Lisa. When you felt me last night, you asked me to come today instead because you wanted to be more rested. You were compelled to Google photos of me to see what I looked like. You didn't like the look of me, did you?

Lisa: Not really. I thought you looked hard and stern and unhappy; that was the energy I was vibing from you.

What do you think of me right now?

Lisa: Well, I did what Jesus told me to do, and I thought of you as nothing more than a part of me. So that even if I was perceiving correctly what you would have been like as a living person, I knew I simply had to look at those very qualities in myself and then learn to love and accept them. So

169

that is what I am working on right now.

I apologize if I am judging incorrectly based on appearance. I know that people misjudged me a lot in my own life, and I don't want to do that to you, Jane.

I accept your apology. I was quite serious in life, and I carried a hardness within me. I was always defensive. I didn't want anyone getting the better of me, so I kept some armor around me, you might say. I was not all that comfortable with softness and vulnerability. I thought it was a weakness and something I should not feel much of, let alone, show to the world at large.

It was a time when women had to fight for everything: respect, admiration, wages, and authority. I wanted to hold my own and show others that I could do that. Not so unlike you, correct? Only you live in a time of almost complete equality, at least where you reside.

Lisa: Yes, I too feel like you did. I don't want to let anyone "pull one over on me" and so I have my boxing gloves on. I'd say that they're more "Golden Gloves" that I have on now, though. I would love to take them off altogether. But to do that, I will need to trust more—especially men. I have issues with that. I think it comes from many of my past lives in which men hurt and killed me. I believe I came into this lifetime remembering that and even though in this lifetime, I have had only very nice, kind, sweet men around me, I still carry the idea or belief that men aren't to be trusted. It's time to let that go, and I have been working toward that end.

Yes, I understand completely. I carried some similar baggage around with me too. I was always on the lookout for anyone trying to overpower me, in business and in personal matters. It was a heavy load to carry, one that really never let me become too comfortable with, or trusting of, certain situations and certain people.

I see now what a waste of time that was, perceiving things that way. I could be so protective, suspicious, guarded—and for what? What I needed was to be warmer, softer, and more vulnerable—and if I had been "taken," I'd still have been better off in the long run, because what a difference that would have made in my life, the quality of my life, and my relationships with others.

But live and learn—I'm amusing myself here. And laughing very loudly! I really DID live and learn; I lived there and am learning here. Now, I don't mean to suggest that there is no learning there, where you are, but most of what we learn there is incorrect. It's just incorrect. It's garbage, Lisa, just garbage. It's a waste of time, learning almost anything there.

What I am seeing here in this place is the expansiveness. It's amazing! Everything goes on forever and ever. Here, we just know things. I don't know how that is possible, but it just is. I don't feel like I am *learning* so much as absorbing what is around me. I just know that what I am absorbing is correct. It feels so good, Lisa. It's not hand-me-down information like it was on Earth, which although it was incorrect from the start, kept getting passed down from generation to generation. No, not at all.

It's a joy to be here, truly a joy! I love what I am being shown—or rather, what I am exposed to here. The energy of everything just fills me up around here. Imagine your entire being just filled up with beauty and music and knowledge and softness and peace. It's ecstasy. I can hardly find words to describe what surrounds and fills me. "Heaven" is a good word, what you would imagine Heaven to be like, but oh, so much better!

I had a lot of fear around Heaven while I was on Earth. I was afraid to find out what was here. I worried how I would be judged here. I definitely believed I would be judged, and let me tell you, I didn't think I would do well. It's hard to be perfect on Earth! But oh, how surprised I was to find out that not only are there no judgments—none whatsoever— it is just the most incredibly blissful place to be. For everyone. No one need ever worry about judgment. It's just amazing! It's as if we leave all of our fear and strife and struggle and anger and pettiness, all such negativity, at the door of this place. We enter into a glorious sanctuary, a golden land of milk and honey, you could say. It's complete love and peace here. And the beings and the atmosphere and all aspects of this place support more love and peace, if that is possible.

I am going to fill you with a bit of what I am experiencing here, if that's OK, Lisa. Sit still and I will share it with you, OK?

Lisa: OK, thank you. I could feel some of it while I was typing, so I'll appreciate getting the full experience of it, for sure.

[I stopped typing so I could take a moment to feel the energy she wanted to share with me. It was glorious!]

Lisa: That was the most beautiful experience, Jane. Thank you so much. It felt like I was being held in the arms of the Divine Mother. It felt positively glorious, as I floated in the vibration of peace and comfort and love. It was unbelievable. I can see why everyone loves it!

I wanted you to feel it as I do so that you could have a reference point for how things are supposed to feel. Remember this feeling, and even while you are in your present state of existence, try to invoke it often.

Soften up, Lisa. Let that playful, free-spirited nature of yours rule your heart. Lead with that. That way, all of your relationships with others will naturally be deeper, sweeter, and more loving. Let your fear go and enter into the grace of this Heaven while you are still on Earth. I wish someone had showed up in my life to teach me what's what. My life would have been far richer than it was, but I didn't have that advantage. I did my best and I think I did quite well in many areas of my life. I just carried a little too much fear around with me, is all. I had fear of people and their intentions, so I kept them a good distance away. That was my solution, but it was not a very good one, I see now. If you can learn from my experience, if anyone can learn from it, then that's marvelous.

I want to send love now to my family, to my children, and to all those I did let in. I feel so much love for you, each one of you. I am beaming down love onto all of you. I'm showering each of you with my pure love. I hope you can feel it, dear darlings.

[*I could feel such profound love wash over and throughout my entire being. I sat basking in this gorgeous energy as she faded into heavenly Light. It was beautiful.*]

Abraham Lincoln et al.

June 16, 2015 — *A Fond Farewell*

[*I started crying, not a heavy sort of crying, more of a sentimental love-connection crying.*]

Lisa, we are complete here. We have accomplished what we set out to do.

Lisa: What is it that you wanted to accomplish, Abe?

We wanted to bring little rays of hope from Heaven down to your world. We shared our hearts and our stories with each of you in an effort to bridge the gap between Heaven and Earth, between life and death, between truth and untruth. We hope that by connecting our worlds, all may benefit in some way.

We are all here. Everyone has gathered around in a big circle, holding hands to symbolize our connectivity to one another. We know here that we are connected, just as we are connected to you down there. Whether you see it with your human eyes or not, you are all connected to one another and to us here, as well.

[It was too late to continue so I had to stop for the night. I assured Abe that I would be available to him and the group the next day, whenever they wished.]

June 18, 2015

All the faces that we wore down there were just that: faces. Not one of those faces was truly us. Not one of the faces that you people are wearing right now is you. It is just a temporary role that you are playing, a costume, and at the end of your life, you will discard that costume like a pair of worn-out shoes, and completely free yourselves from the identification of that role.

Can you understand how little importance must be placed on that particular role you are playing? Enjoy it; go ahead. You're in it, playing it, so most certainly get into the character and live it for the experience of it. But for heaven's sake, do not believe yourselves to BE that. You are not the mother, or the teacher, or the victim, or the artist, or the activist. You are the essence of Love, the Divine manifestation of the living God. You will leave that character behind and never play it again. Please realize that. The only thing that you will wish for when you shed that worn-out costume is to be once again reunited with Source, the Divine Light. You will see yourselves as only energetic Light, just as you will see everyone else.

That is why we have chosen to express to you more of our true selves for this project. Yes, we referenced our lives and loves on Earth, but we chose not to discuss in too much detail our lives there as those were simply "our roles." It was not then, nor is it now, who we are.

We wanted to visit with you and share a little of our experience behind the veil. We wanted to speak to you of the important things within us now, the things that are real to us now. We are sharing from a different perspective. We are all in various places and stages, and our experiences differ; that is as it should be. There is more than one reality here, as there, and we are sharing ours with each of you. As we evolve and grow in Light, we know and live more of the ultimate truth.

Light is knowledge. Inside the Light, you will find truth. Seek the Light, therefore, if you wish to know truth.

Everyone is here, gathered around, to thank you for your help in bridging our two worlds. We so much appreciate your willingness to deliver our messages. We hope our individual and collective messages help bring people closer to the Light. If it does, then that will be our greatest contribution to Earths' people.

We have more guests here, lined up, ready to speak with you, Lisa, but what has been given to you so far is ready to be shared with the world.

We have much gratitude for you and for everyone who reads our words.

Blessings, dear Lisa.

[*I could see Marilyn just swaying to and fro, as if there were some beautiful music playing that I could not hear. She was smiling, a peaceful, sweet, gentle smile, and looking pleased. George, standing next to Jesus, had an enormous smile on his face; it was radiant. Waylon was kicking at the imaginary ground, looking at me with a cute, coy smile, like he had a secret. Paul, with his hand on his heart, was imploring me with his eyes to deliver his message, like he would hold his breath until it was done, like he would stand still and do nothing else until it was safely delivered to his loved ones. I could feel the enormous gratitude in his big heart. A feeling of pure love filled my heart and brought more tears to my eyes. Cleopatra was holding her arm up as if to say, "Charge!" She was conveying strength and power in the way she stood, and in her very energy. That is what she wanted represented and shared. Elvis and Michael, stood with their heads bowed. I felt some sadness in them, and yet I could see that their load had been lightened, just by their having shared.*

Those were the guests who had stepped forward for me to see and feel clearly. All the rest hung back, in a big semicircle, facing me. They looked very content and at peace, as a group. I let this feeling of peace wash over me. It was incredibly beautiful. I remained still for a moment to bask in this glowing wave of Light.

I clasped my hands together in prayer position and nodded my head to the group, silently acknowledging and thanking each of them. They returned the blessing. It was a beautiful moment for me.

Then, with their hands remaining in prayer position, they backed away, seeming to not want to turn their backs on me. They faded into the Light as they went. I felt a sense of sadness as I watched them go, wishing I had more time with each of them, and yet I felt deeply blessed by our time together.]

I hope you've enjoyed reading my book

and that the messages have touched your life in some meaningful way.

As a special thank you for purchasing my book, I would like to offer you some exciting **FREE GIFTS** that may further help you on this path of self-growth and enlightenment. It is also my hope that this will allow us to stay in touch so that should you ever find yourself asking bigger questions, you will be able to easily find me! As an international psychic/medium, I would love to help you get "Tomorrow's Answers – Today"!

To receive your free gifts, please visit:
www.dyingtotellyoubooks.com

You will receive:

+ FREE MOVIE! Watch "What If? The Movie" and live your full potential now!

+ FREE TIP GUIDE! How to Increase Your Intuitive IQ

+ FREE INTUITIVE READING! Enter to Win (A New Winner Drawn Each Month)!

+ Exciting COURSE SPECIALS!

You may reach out to me personally for a reading or just to say hello at:

• Email: lisa@dyingtotellyoubooks.com

• Twitter: https://twitter.com/dyingtotellyou1

• Facebook: https://www.facebook.com/dyingtotellyoubooks/

• LinkedIn: https://www.linkedin.com/in/dyingtotellyoubooks/

Made in the USA
Coppell, TX
24 April 2021

54461869R00105